CW00557708

Ukraine and European Security

CHATHAM HOUSE PAPERS

A Russia and Eurasia Programme Publication
Programme Head: Roy Allison

The Royal Institute of International Affairs, at Chatham House in London, has provided an impartial forum for discussion and debate on current international issues for over 75 years. Its resident research fellows, specialized information resources, and range of publications, conferences, and meetings span the fields of international politics, economics, and security. The Institute is independent of government.

Chatham House Papers are short monographs on current policy problems which have been commissioned by the RIIA. In preparing the papers, authors are advised by a study group of experts convened by the RIIA, and publication of a paper indicates that the Institute regards it as an authoritative contribution to the public debate. The Institute does not, however, hold opinions of its own; the views expressed in this publication are the responsibility of the author.

CHATHAM HOUSE PAPERS

Ukraine and European Security

Tor Bukkvoll

THE ROYAL INSTITUTE
OF INTERNATIONAL
AFFAIRS

Pinter
A Cassell Imprint
Wellington House, 125 Strand, London WC2R 0BB, United Kingdom

First published in 1997

© Royal Institute of International Affairs, 1997

British Library Cataloguing in Publication Data
A CIP catalogue record for this book is available from the British Library

Library of Congress Cataloging in Publication Data
A CIP catalogue record for this book is available from the Library of Congress

ISBN 1-85567-465-3 (Paperback)
       1-85567-464-5 (Hardback)

Typeset by Koinonia Limited
Printed and bound in Great Britain by
Biddles Limited, Guildford and King's Lynn

Contents

Contents

Acknowledgments

First of all I would like to thank the Norwegian Ministry of Defence for generously providing the financial support for this project. Further funding was provided by the Volkswagen Foundation as part of the joint project of the Royal Institute of International Affairs and the Bundesinstitut für ostwissenschaftliche und internationale Studien (BIOst), Cologne, on 'European Security and the Post-Soviet States'. I am also indebted to many people for the completion of this paper. A special word of appreciation is due to my colleague Sven Gunnar Simonsen, for all the help and advice he gave me during the project. My thanks go also to Pål Kolstø and Anatoliy Yamskov, who have commented upon different parts of the paper. I am particularly indebted to Dr Pavel Baev at the International Peace Research Institute (PRIO), Oslo, for his support, and because he always detects the logical mistakes in any manuscript; the section on civil–military relations has been written in collaboration with him. PRIO Director Dan Smith and all his colleagues at the Institute also deserve particular mention, for making PRIO such a stimulating place to work. I would further like to thank the Institute of Global and Regional Security in Kiev, which provided vital assistance during my stay in Ukraine; Roy Allison and members of the study group at the RIIA for their advice and good suggestions; and Sarah Peasley and Gillian Bromley for their editorial help.

Oslo,   Tor Bukkvoll
January 1997

Abbreviations

ACC	Arab Cooperation Council
ACV	armed combat vehicle
BSF	Black Sea Fleet
CCU	Civic Congress of Ukraine
CFE	Conventional Forces in Europe
CIS	Commonwealth of Independent States
CSCE	Conference on Security and Cooperation in Europe (now OSCE)
CUN	Congress of Ukrainian Nationalists
DPU	Democratic Party of Ukraine
ESU	eastern and southern Ukraine
FIC	financial-industrial conglomerate
FNPU	Federation of Independent Ukrainian Trade Unions
IMF	International Monetary Fund
NATO	North Atlantic Treaty Organization
NMCT	National Movement of Crimean Tatars
NPT	[Nuclear] Non-Proliferation Treaty
OCNM	Organization of the Crimean Tatar National Movement
OSCE	Organization for Security and Cooperation in Europe (formerly CSCE)
OVPU	Union of Free Trade Unions
PDPU	People's Democratic Party of Ukraine
PDRU	Party of Democratic Rebirth of Ukraine
PER(C)	Party for Economic Renaissance [of Crimea]
PSPU	Progressive Socialist Party of Ukraine
RMC	Republican Movement of Crimea
SPU	Socialist Party of Ukraine

START   Strategic Arms Reduction Talks/Treaty
SUP   Slavic Unity Party
UNA   Ukrainian National Assembly
UNSO   Ukrainian National Self-Defence
UOCK   Ukrainian Orthodox Church of the Kiev Patriarchate
URP   Ukrainian Republican Party
USRC   Union for the Support of the Republic of Crimea
UUO   Union of Ukrainian Officers
UWC   Ukrainian Workers' Congress
WEU   Western European Union

Map of Ukraine

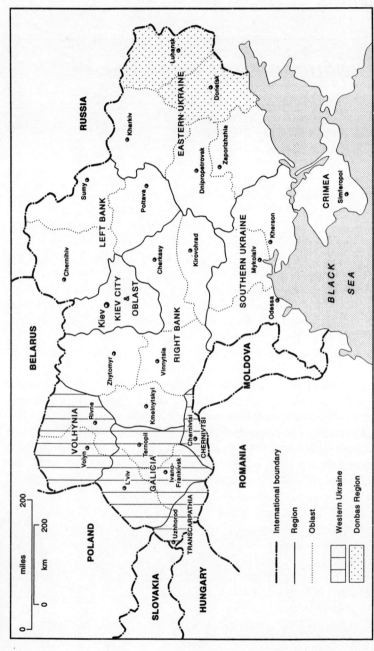

© Andrew Wilson, 1996. Adapted from Wilson, *Ukrainian Nationalism in the 1990s* (Cambridge University Press, 1996).

Chapter 1

Introduction

Ukraine has been called 'Europe's linchpin', and 'a strategic pivot in Europe'.[1] In April 1996 Xavier Solana, Secretary-General of NATO, stated that Ukraine 'has an absolutely unique role to play in securing stability on the continent'.[2] Why has Ukraine come to be considered such an important country for the future of European security? Three reasons stand out as central: Ukrainian independence is a defining feature of the future European security architecture; Ukraine is a crucial determinant in the formation of the future Russia; and it is considered a potential candidate for serious ethnic conflict and separatism.

Ukraine is one of the defining features of the European security architecture because the existence of an independent, non-aligned Ukraine creates a stabilizing geographical distance between Russia on the one side and east-central and western Europe on the other. If that distance were to disappear, the consequences for European security politics could be serious. Ukraine's strategic position is cast into particularly sharp focus by the current process of NATO expansion. The present NATO policy of not deploying nuclear weapons and foreign combat troops on the territories of the prospective NATO members in eastern and central Europe might have to be revised if Ukraine came under Russia's control, and Moscow, for example, took the opportunity to station troops in Ukraine. Similarly, if Ukraine applied to become and was accepted as a member of NATO, Russia might deem this a strategic loss of such major proportions as to warrant preventative military action to stop it. Michael Mandelbaum has argued in *Foreign Affairs* that it 'is not an exaggeration to say that NATO expansion will be good or bad depending on its effect on the peaceful coexistence of Ukraine and Russia'.[3]

Ukraine is crucial in determining the future nature of Russia, as the

1

litmus test of Russia's willingness to accept the independence of its former possessions. For Russia this is a question both of identity and of control. Fully to accept Ukrainian independence implies a redefinition of what Russia is, and it also implies losing control over territories of vital strategic importance to Russia. If Russia turns out not to be willing to accept Ukrainian independence, and tries to subordinate parts of it, the inevitable conflict that will ensue between the two states will hamper their democratization, because authoritarian rule might be necessary to keep an unwilling Ukraine from seceding from a position of subordination. An authoritarian Russia, aggressively guarding its control over Ukraine, could become a troublesome negotiating partner for the rest of Europe, and the negotiation of future security arrangements for Europe could be jeopardized by such an outcome.

Ethnic conflict and separatism in Ukraine would have consequences for the security of the rest of Europe. Serious ethnic conflict could easily involve Russia, thus risking escalation into interstate conflict. If Russia then managed to gain control over Ukraine, it could eliminate the geographical distance between itself and east-central and western Europe. Even if the conflict were confined to Ukrainian territory, the Yugoslav example shows the impact such a crisis can have on European security. Millions of refugees, considerable domestic political pressure in other countries for the involvement of military forces in trying to stop bloodshed, the potential failure of such efforts and disagreements over how to conduct them: all these experiences have been dearly bought from the Yugoslav crisis.

Bearing in mind these security considerations, this study focuses on three features of independent Ukraine: the evolution of democracy; the potential of ethnic Russian-based anti-independence mobilization; and the troubled Ukrainian–Russian relationship. Whether Ukraine becomes a stable democracy is likely to have an impact both on its relationship with Russia and on the potential of ethnic mobilization. Democratic regimes are less prone to fight wars and commonly experience fewer ethnic conflicts than do non-democratic regimes.[4]

Chapter 2 outlines the main events of Ukrainian high politics since independence and then considers whether Ukrainian democracy is being consolidated or not. This is done by evaluating Ukraine according to attitudinal, behavioural and constitutional indicators of democratic consolidation.[5] The chapter concludes that although it is still only a democratizing rather than a fully democratic state, developments in Ukraine demonstrate, with few exceptions, that the country is moving in the direction of stable democracy.

Chapter 3 investigates the potential for ethnic mobilization among Russians in eastern and southern Ukraine and Crimea. After accounting for anti-independence activity in these regions, its main emphasis is on explaining why the Russians of eastern and southern Ukraine have not mobilized, whereas the Russians of Crimea have. In eastern and southern Ukraine the Russian-based anti-independence movements have argued essentially for a restoration of something like the former Soviet Union. While this idea is not alien either to Russians or to Russified Ukrainians in eastern and southern Ukraine, the anti-independence movements here have attracted very few followers. In Crimea, by contrast, the emphasis has been on separation rather than restoration, and here popular support has been plentiful. Nevertheless, in Crimea, too, the separatist drive seems to be in decline after a peak of activity in 1994–5.

Chapter 4 examines Ukraine's crucial relationship with Russia. Although Ukraine's relations with the West, east-central Europe and its southern neighbours are also discussed, it is this bilateral relationship that is central to non-European security. The chapter presents four scenarios for the future development of the Ukrainian–Russian relationship. Finally, Chapter 5 presents a summary of the findings of the study.

A politically stable Ukraine at peace with its neighbours is fundamental to peace and stability in Europe. This study is an attempt to highlight some of the central factors influencing such an outcome.

Chapter 2

The evolution of Ukrainian democracy

This chapter has two purposes: to introduce the reader to the Ukrainian political scene, and to assess how far democracy has been consolidated in Ukraine. It starts with a general outline of the interplay between the main actors in Ukrainian politics since independence, and then looks at the spectrum of political parties. It argues that Ukraine is on its way to consolidating democracy: both the population and the political elite accept democratic rules of the game; non-democratic forces are weak in Ukrainian society; and major political conflicts are solved through compromise rather than violent action.

Politics since independence

The nomenklatura–national-democratic alliance (1990–94)

From 1990 to 1994 Ukraine was ruled by representatives of the Ukrainian nomenklatura and the Communist Party, turned nationalist, in cooperation with western and central Ukrainian moderate nationalists from the former opposition.

The 1990 Ukrainian parliament was elected at a time when the Communist Party was still able to secure a majority of the seats. Of the 450 seats, the Communists gained 239, the opposition about 130, and the rest went to independent representatives. At that time most of the opposition in parliament was united under the umbrella of the moderately nationalist Rukh movement (see below). The parliament thus had a Communist majority when Ukraine became independent in 1991.

Given the small numerical representation of what was called the democratic block in parliament, one might easily conclude that the block was not very influential. This conclusion, however, seems to be premature. The representatives of the democratic block were elected on non-

4

communist political platforms that already incorporated concepts of independent state-building. These concepts had largely been formulated by the so-called *shestydesyatnyki* (those from the Sixties):[1] that is, those who belonged to the Ukrainian dissident movement that became active in the 1960s (especially the Ukrainian Helsinki Group). Their ideology was a mixture of Ukrainian nationalism and emphasis on human rights. When Ukraine gained independence in 1991, the former Communists had no ready-made concepts in the creation of Ukrainian foreign, ethnic or nation-building policies, since all their political activity had taken place within the framework of a different regime and in a different country. The choice facing them was therefore whether to accept and adopt what was presented to them by the opposition, to develop their own new concepts, or to cling to nostalgia for the old system. What happened was that the concepts of the nationalist opposition were adopted to varying degrees by both Leonid Kravchuk, elected Ukrainian president in December 1991, and a substantial proportion of the former Communists. They also adopted several of the opposition members themselves: many national democrats from Rukh and the Ukrainian Republican Party, most of them from western Ukraine, rose to power under Kravchuk.

Why did the Communists adopt the nationalist discourse rather than any other?[2] The cognitive distance between the old communist discourse and the new nationalist discourse can help in answering this question, since a number of similar basic assumptions or ways of thinking can be identified.

First, they both emphasize the need for a strong state. In the 'Complex Programme for Social-Economic Reform' published in the national-democratic political theoretical journal *Rozbudova Derzhavy*, it is stressed that 'it is a dangerous illusion to think that authentic democracy is connected with weak state structures'.[3] Since the former communists had worked for most of their life within a discourse where the state was everything, this stance was probably easy to accept.

Second, there is a tendency in both discourses to seek 'final solutions', as opposed to 'process solutions' with no certain end. Oleksandr Mayboroda, in an article on Ukrainian nationality policy, exemplifies this similarity: 'As in the former system [read: communist discourse], the new political forces [read: national-democratic discourse] sincerely believe in their ability to finally solve the national problem, achieve a permanent harmony in the relationship between nationalities ... forgetting that national antagonisms are an inevitable and eternal companion for a multi-national state.'[4]

5

Third, there is in both discourses an inclination to put political priorities before economic priorities. Just as Soviet propaganda urged the population to make sacrifices for the sake of a bright communist future, Ukrainians are now exhorted to endure economic difficulties resulting from a decline in trade with Russia, since this decline in trade helps Ukraine to distance itself from Russia; the sacrifices will be rewarded by the consolidation of Ukrainian independence. The basis of legitimacy for the political regime thus becomes commitment to the cause, not economic and social satisfaction. The 'Ukrainian political economy of nationalism' was, according to an observer of Ukrainian politics, different from the political economy of socialism only in that 'While the political economy of socialism after all was based on some kind of economic calculations, the political economy of nationalism does not recognize any other foundations than the emotional ones.'[5]

Fourth, there is in both discourses a disposition towards 'politics by proclamations' and 'illusionism'– that is, an appreciation of big words and grand projects as opposed to politics understood as a process of incremental solutions sought through immediate and not always glorious tasks. According to Oleksandr Shmorhun, this tendency, which he calls 'political idealism', developed under the old regime and is essential to understanding politics throughout the former USSR. Shmorhun criticizes this political idealism not only for its way of focusing on politics, but also for its 'total loss of connection with reality, and ever growing illusion that numerous declarations, resolutions and conferences by themselves will change things for the better'.[6] The political observer Sergeiy Tikhii saw the same phenomenon in the Kravchuk leadership's determination to turn Ukrainian foreign policy as much as possible towards the West. According to him, the Ukrainian political leadership reasoned thus: 'The West is unwilling to open its doors for us. It doesn't matter, we will just keep on knocking and knocking, and in the end they will open their doors.'[7] They assumed that declaration after declaration, instead of improved economic performance, was the way to open the doors to the West.

Fifth, there is in both discourses a strong drive for unity in society. In the Soviet communist discourse it was repeatedly stated that collective interests stand above individual interests. The influential national-democratic ideologist Larisa Skorik also urged the need to 'renounce personal ambitions, rise above one's own sentiments and the interests of parties and groups, in the understanding that state-building is only accomplished by the strong and tightly organized'.[8]

Essentially, then, the Ukrainian nomenklatura was forced by the turn of events to find a new ideological basis for its continued exercise of power. The moderate nationalist discourse of the *shestydesiatniky* was found to be the most suitable for explaining Ukrainian independence, and not very difficult for former Communists to assimilate.

Communists and pragmatists from eastern Ukraine (1994–)
The March 1994 parliamentary elections and the July 1994 presidential elections swept the nomenklatura–national-democratic alliance out of power in Kiev. The March elections brought a left-wing majority to the Ukrainian parliament. The left-wing parties had done particularly well in populous eastern and southern Ukraine. However, substantial defections of originally left-wing candidates to more moderate parliamentary factions, and success for the moderates in 1994 by-elections, gradually eroded this majority. The parliament in 1996 consists of four major groupings: the left, the national democrats and nationalists, the pro-reform moderates, and the *bolota* (the 'swamp') – representatives who sometimes support the left and sometimes the national democrats and pro-reform moderates.

The national democrats and the pro-reform moderates have been the main parliamentary supporters of Leonid Kuchma since he became president in July 1994. However, to achieve a majority in parliament for his policy proposals, Kuchma has needed to attract a sufficient number of votes from the *bolota*, and to a large extent he has succeeded. It is therefore fair to speak of a change in Ukrainian politics since his election as president. This change can be summed up as a move from a combination of nation-building and absence of economic reform under Kravchuk, to a combination of pragmatism and initiation of economic reform under Kuchma. Both presidents have, however, had to deal with not very cooperative parliaments when trying to get their policies through.

The distribution of power
The distribution of power is normally decided by a country's constitution. In Ukraine the old constitution was made for a political system that no longer existed after independence. The delineation of power in the period since independence was therefore regulated by amendments to the existing constitution, thus opening the way for more rapid shifts in the rules of the game than would have been possible under normal constitutional rule.

Kravchuk from the beginning argued that a strong executive was necessary to secure independence. This opinion seems to have been

7

widely shared in parliament, which on 14 February 1992 granted Kravchuk the right to issue decrees having the force of law, appoint ministers directly and appoint his own representatives in each district in Ukraine. These local representatives' decisions were to be binding for local government. Eleven days later, without any constitutional foundation, he established the State Council, whose decisions had to be formally debated in different political fora at the central level. It is noteworthy that all except one of the members of the State Council came from Rukh. Though these actions clearly meant a strong concentration of power in the hands of the president, they were all accepted by the parliament.

These developments took a new turn on 20 May 1993, when Kravchuk unexpectedly asked the parliament to make him head of government, and to eliminate the post of prime minister. This request was also justified by reference to the need for a strong executive. Leonid Kuchma, then prime minister, had already announced that he would resign if the special rights he had received in economic decision-making were not renewed and extended. Thus both the prime minister and the president were asking the parliament for additional powers on the basis of the need for a strong executive. The parliament reacted by rejecting the president's proposition, and at the same time depriving Kuchma of his special powers and refusing to accept his resignation.

When Kuchma became president in July 1994 Yerhen Marchuk was appointed prime minister, accepting that this role was subordinate to the president's. But the tug of war over spheres of authority between the president and the parliament continued. Kuchma accused the parliament of blocking his attempts at economic reform, and the parliament accused Kuchma of trying to rule the country like a dictator. In June 1995, in an attempt to end the confrontation Kuchma announced a referendum on trust in the president and trust in the parliament. In a parliamentary initiative to avoid the referendum, 240 deputies, together with the president, signed a so-called 'constitutional agreement' which was to regulate the spheres of authority until a new constitution could be adopted. The agreement was a compromise, giving Kuchma more authority than he had but less then he wanted; it reduced tensions between the two sides, but there continued to be conflicts over its interpretation. The agreement was to remain in force for one year, after which a new constitution, prepared by a special commission, was to be adopted.

In spring 1996 the constitutional process became the main political battleground in Ukraine. Several projects were discussed in parliament, and 'compromise-seeking' commissions were set up to try to find a common platform. The main bones of contention were the delineation of the respective powers of president, government and parliament; the degree of local self-government, especially in Crimea; the state symbols – flag, coat of arms, anthem and state language; and the principle of private property. The main line of confrontation separated the left-wing forces of the parliament on one side from the moderates, national democrats and president on the other, with the *bolota* supporting either side depending on the article in question. Those supporting most of President Kuchma's positions were in the majority, but had to win over members of the *bolota* and the left to secure the 300 votes necessary to adopt each article of the constitution.

After many lengthy debates, the constitution was adopted as a whole on 28 June 1996, with 315 votes in favour and 36 against. As a result, the status of private property was secured, Crimea retained its right to an autonomous status above *oblast* level, Russian did not become a second state language, the blue and yellow flag and the trident remained the Ukrainian state symbols, and the president retained the right to appoint the government. However, the government has to be accepted by the parliament.

The main reason why the constitution was adopted was the threat of a referendum. Early in 1996 President Kuchma warned the parliament that if it proved unable to adopt the constitution, he would try to have it adopted by referendum. This was a real threat to the anti-Kuchma forces in parliament, since the text that would have been put to the vote in such a referendum would have been one formulated by experts loyal to the president, therefore clearly favouring the presidency. If Kuchma had won such a referendum – which was quite possible – the anti-Kuchma forces would have lost their chance of negotiating a better deal by adopting the constitution in parliament. When on 26 June both the National Security Council and the Council of Regions called for a referendum, on the grounds that the absence of a constitution posed a threat to Ukrainian political stability, the pressure on parliament came to a head. The parliamentary factions therefore showed themselves more willing to compromise than they had ever been before. The national democrats accepted the autonomous status of Crimea, and in return the leftists accepted the blue and yellow flag and the trident. One of the more curious compromises was that the leftists accepted the tune but not the text of the national anthem. The text is therefore to be decided by an all-Ukrainian competition.

Survey of political forces

During the period since independence four main strands of Ukrainian political parties have developed: the national democrats, the moderates, the leftist parties and the radical nationalists. The following survey is not exhaustive; it deals only with the most important parties within each strand.

The national democrats

Rukh Rukh was founded in September 1989. From then until spring 1992 it was the main opposition force in Ukraine. It was from the outset not a political party but rather a broad-based 'umbrella organization' of political parties, cultural organizations and others, all united against the Communist regime and in favour of Ukrainian independence. At its third congress in March 1992, a split occurred between those who preferred to stay in opposition to President Kravchuk, led by Vyacheslav Chornovil, and those who took the view that in this critical period of establishing independence it was necessary to support President Kravchuk, led by Myhailo Horyn and Ivan Dratch. A compromise was, however, forced through at the congress by a representative of the Ukrainian diaspora in the West, whereby all three were elected joint leaders of Rukh. The representative of the Ukrainian diaspora could do this because Rukh's activity was to a great extent financed by the diaspora. The collective leadership did not work, however: Dratch pulled out and Horyn became leader of the Ukrainian Republican Party, and at Rukh's fourth congress in December 1992 Chornovil was elected as the sole leader of Rukh. Rukh was officially registered as an ordinary political party in February 1993.

Politically, Rukh can be characterized as a centre-right party. It works for Western-style democracy and market economics, and puts special emphasis on questions of Ukrainian rebirth: consolidating independence, strengthening the position of the Ukrainian language and Ukrainian culture, etc. It also argues for the immediate withdrawal of Ukraine from the Commonwealth of Independent States (CIS).

In the Ukrainian parliamentary elections of 1994, Rukh fared badly, winning only 27 seats. These representatives constitute a separate faction in the parliament.

The Ukrainian Republican Party (URP) and the Democratic Party of Ukraine (DPU)

The URP was established in April 1990 by the famous Ukrainian dissident Levko Lukyanenko, who had spent 26 years in Soviet prisons. It took only nine seats in the 1994 elections. The DPU was established in December 1990. It is viewed as a party of intellectuals and is led by the charismatic Volodymyr Yavorivsky. It took just six seats in the 1994 elections. Together with several independent deputies and other more radical nationalists from UNA-UNSO (The Ukrainian National Assembly and Ukrainian National Self-Defence – see below) and CUN (Congress of Ukrainian Nationalists), these two parties formed the parliamentary faction Derzhavnist (Statehood), which is supported by 28 deputies. Ideologically, URP and DPU are both close to Rukh on most major issues.

The moderates

New Ukraine (centre-left) The New Ukraine block was formed in June 1992. Its main initiator, the Party of Democratic Rebirth of Ukraine (PDRU), was established in December 1990 on the basis of the so-called Democratic Platform that broke away from the Communist Party. Together with two social-democratic parties, the Green Party and many other groupings, the PDRU tried to make New Ukraine into the main force in the 1990–94 parliament promoting market reform. Among the other organizations in New Ukraine were the Ukrainian League of Companies with Foreign Capital, the Ukrainian Confederation of Industrialists and some trade unions. The social democrats later left New Ukraine, and after 1993 the block gradually lost its dominant position within the moderate camp to the Liberal Party of Ukraine. In July 1995, however, there were attempts at a revival of New Ukraine, in which several leading Ukrainian politicians, for example the deputy speaker of the parliament, Oleg Demin, and former presidential adviser Valeriy Pustovoytenko, took prominent positions. In February 1996 the driving forces behind New Ukraine, PDRU and the Ukrainian Workers' Congress (UWC), decided to merge the three bodies into a new political party, the People's Democratic Party of Ukraine (PDPU). This has left New Ukraine in a very unclear situation. It is not disbanded, but it has become increasingly clear that work within New Ukraine will be given little priority by the PDRU and UWC elements in the PDPU.

The Liberal Party of Ukraine (centre-right) The Liberal Party of Ukraine was established in Donetsk in 1991 by the local businessman Ihor Markulov. Its social base was at the outset limited to eastern Ukraine, but by summer 1995 the party had developed an all-Ukrainian profile. Support from business circles means that party finances are solid, and a number of prominent Ukrainian politicians, including the former Ukrainian president Leonid Kravchuk, have either joined the party or declared their affiliation with it. Although the Liberal Party did not win a single seat in the 1994 parliamentary elections, its has been able to organize a group of twelve deputies into the Market Choice parliamentary faction.

During spring 1996 there were persistent rumours of a forthcoming merger between the Liberal Party and two other centre-right parties: the Party of Economic Recovery* and the Interregional Block for Reforms.

In economic policy New Ukraine has a social-democratic orientation, whereas the Liberal Party is of a more liberal tendency. Both, however, seem increasingly to have moved closer to the national democrats on questions of Ukrainian independence and statehood. At its fourth congress in July 1995 New Ukraine came out in favour of a unitarian – as opposed to a federal – state structure, and of Ukrainian as the country's only state language. In January 1995 the Liberal Party chose the outspoken defender of Ukrainian statehood, Oleh Soskin, as its leader. His political views were, however, hard to accept for the party's eastern and southern Ukrainian majority, and in May 1995 he resigned as party leader. The new leader of the Liberal Party was Volodymyr Shcherban, chairman of the *oblast* council of Donetsk.

The left parties
The Socialist Party of Ukraine The Socialist Party of Ukraine (SPU) was established in October 1991 after the Communist Party had been banned as a result of the failed Soviet coup. Its political programme was originally in favour of a return to the past, to a planned economy, to abolition of the multi-party system and a renewed federation with the republics of the former Soviet Union. It has since moderated its position on most of these issues, and is today advocating a mixed economy with strong social guarantees, and an independent Ukraine in close cooperation with the other former Soviet republics. The Socialist Party took 26 seats in the

---

* This party was earlier called the Party for the Economic Recovery of Crimea, and was a regional Crimean party, but in March 1996 it officially became an all-Ukrainian party, and changed its name to the Party of Economic Recovery.

1994 parliamentary elections, and its leader is the Parliamentary Speaker, Aleksandr Moroz.

At the SPU's third congress in February 1996 a small core of orthodox Marxists left the party because, according to them, it had 'adopted social-liberal positions'.[9] These Marxists, led by Natalya Vitrenko and Volodymyr Marchenko, later established the Progressive Socialist Party of Ukraine (PSPU).

The Communist Party of Ukraine The Communist Party of Ukraine re-emerged on the Ukrainian political scene only in October 1993, but soon became a political success story. In a short time it re-established its organizational structures, and it now has local branches in all *oblasts* and most large and medium-sized towns. In the 1994 parliamentary elections the Communist Party gained the largest number of seats of any single party – 87. A major weakness, however, is that most of its support is among older people. Although a member of the party's presidium, Yevgeniy Marmazov, reacted to remarks about the average age of party supporters by retorting 'pensioners are not enemies',[10] it is a problem for any political party to appeal almost only to older people.

The Communist Party advocates closer cooperation with the other former Soviet republics. It accepts all forms of property, but states that priority should be given to collectively owned property. In questions of Ukrainian statehood it has, however, increasingly been forced to take into account the position of Communists in western and central Ukraine. The party is split over the status of the Russian language, and has had to accept that Ukraine should be a sovereign state. Its unity may also be under threat on questions of economic reform. According to Victor Musiyaka, a deputy from the pro-reform *Reformy* (Reforms) parliamentary faction, the present Communist parliamentary grouping consists of one part ideologically motivated old-time communists and one part pragmatists. Several from the latter group have themselves become considerable owners of property.[11]

The Ukrainian Communists naturally pinned high hopes on a Communist victory in the 1996 Russian presidential elections. Vasiliy Arestov, a Communist activist, said in June 1996 that in the event of a such a victory in Russia, 'Ukraine would become the only black island among red and reddening surroundings', suggesting that such a situation would not last long.[12] Zyuganov's defeat was therefore probably felt as a hard blow by Ukrainian as well as Russian Communists.

Agrarian Party of Ukraine The Agrarian Party was established in the southern Ukrainian city of Kherson in January 1992, as an equivalent to the Socialist Party in the Ukrainian countryside, and to counterbalance the radical nationalistic Ukrainian Democratic Agrarian Party. The agrarians did well in the 1994 elections, gaining 35 seats. However, their parliamentary faction split in two in June 1995, when twenty deputies who were dissatisfied with the faction's anti-reform policy left and established a new parliamentary faction called 'Agrarians For Reform'.

The radical nationalists

In Ukraine, political extremism has been a fairly marginal phenomenon since independence. Most probably it will remain so, but the rise of one extreme group, the Ukrainian National Assembly and its paramilitary wing the Ukrainian National Self-Defence, still merits attention.

On 18 July 1995 Ukraine captured international headlines when Ukrainian riot police brutally dispersed the mourning procession of the late Metropolitan of the Ukrainian Orthodox Church of the Kiev Patriarchate, Volodymyr. When the mourners tried to bury the patriarch under the pavement outside the famous Sofia cathedral – they were forbidden by the Ukrainian authorities to bury him on the cathedral's premises – the police attacked with tear gas and truncheons. The confrontation resulted in a large number of wounded. One of the major organizers of the extraordinary ceremony was UNA-UNSO. Though there are other radical nationalist parties in Ukraine, UNA-UNSO is by far the most prominent. It is still a marginal political force in Ukraine, but its influence and popularity have long been on the rise. The organization also merits special attention because it has created its own paramilitary structures, thus challenging the Ukrainian state's monopoly on coercive force.

UNA-UNSO originally propagated extreme Ukrainian chauvinism, but in autumn 1994 changed its ideology to Ukrainian imperialism, downplaying the ethnic factor. The goals of the post-1994 UNA-UNSO can be summarized as follows:

- A new pan-Slavic Eurasian empire, led by Ukraine, and with its capital in Kiev. Dmytro Korchynsky, ideoogical leader of UNA-UNSO, is promising the Ukrainians an empire because 'our people got used to living in a great power, and UNA will make sure they do not have to change their habits'.[13]
- An authoritarian, non-democratic state. One of their slogans is: 'Vote UNA, and you will be spared from going to the elections again.'[14]

- A state-controlled market economy. The ideal presented in UNA's programme is 'a strong state that honours work, thrift, activity and enterprise'.[15]

Its strategies, too, can be summarized under three headings:

- Gradually weakening the Russian hegemony in the post-Soviet environment by fighting Russia everywhere except on Ukrainian soil. A UNA-UNSO activist told the Ukrainian daily *Nezavisimost* in August 1993: 'Our next step will be to create hot-spots in Russia herself.'[16]
- Gaining political dividends by exploiting the growing social grievances in Ukraine. Oleh Vytovych, the party's chairman, confirmed in November 1994 that it would be concentrating its activities on the 'least socially protected parts of the population'.[17]
- Creating small fighting cells all over Ukraine, ready to assume power locally when the time is ripe.

At least five conditions are facilitating a more prominent role for UNA-UNSO in Ukrainian politics. First, increasing social and economic misery is boosting popular support for it among the most disadvantaged. In the March 1994 parliamentary elections it did surprisingly well in Kiev, particularly in those electoral districts, such as Obolon, that covered the poorest parts of the capital. In western Ukraine, Lviv *oblast* leader Andriy Shkil has instructed UNA-UNSO activists to become involved in social protection, for example providing pensioners with minimum food rations and standing up for individuals against unreasonable local authorities. To move in where the state fails is now becoming a UNA-UNSO strategy. The experience from Muslim countries indicates that protecting the individual when state authorities are unable or unwilling to do so can be a very effective way of increasing popular support.

Second, the change from ethnic Ukrainian nationalism to a more inclusive imperial ideology – with the main emphasis on economic stability and law and order – may broaden the party's support beyond nationally conscious Ukrainians. In May 1994 UNA-UNSO parliamentary deputy Yuriy Tyma confirmed the importance of the inclusive aspect of its ideology: 'We do not divide Ukraine along territorial lines. We strive to unite the Ukrainian people independent of religious confession, ethnicity, nationality or language. We are equally accepted everywhere. By the way, the UNA-UNSO deputies will soon tour eastern Ukraine to demonstrate the unity of the Ukrainian lands.'[18] Such a campaign may strengthen the party's influence also in central and parts of eastern and southern Ukraine, ridding it of the purely western Ukrainian image. This will not be easy, however, since in eastern and southern Ukraine anything political that originated in western Ukraine is regarded with great scepticism.

Third, UNA-UNSO has already targeted the Ukrainian trade unions as promising potential partners. Obtaining a foothold in the trade unions has become a primary goal. In spring 1995 Dmytro Korchynsky declared it a central aim of the party to 'chuck the Communists out of the unions'.[19] There are generally speaking two kinds of trade unions in Ukraine: the successors of the Soviet trade unions, grouped together as the Federation of Independent Ukrainian Trade Unions (FNPU), and the new 'independent' trade unions, most of which are loosely organized in the Union of Free Trade Unions (OVPU). The FNPU still organizes by far the largest part of the workforce, but the independent trade unions are strong in certain key sectors such as coal, the metal industry and transport. UNA-UNSO has made no inroads into the FNPU, but seems to have had some success in the OVPU.

Fourth, there are signs that the gulf of enmity between UNA-UNSO and the national democrats is narrowing. The national democrats earlier condemned UNA-UNSO and thus hampered the latter's recruitment, especially in western and central Ukraine. However, the beating of mourners at the Sofia cathedral on 18 July 1995 and the subsequent ban on UNA by the Ukrainian justice ministry may have initiated a rapprochement. UNA-UNSO activist Anatoly Lupynis said after these events: 'Independent of differing political sentiments, the turn of events forced all champions of the realization of Ukrainian state independence to recognize that UNA-UNSO is the vanguard of the Ukrainian national energy. Therefore, on the nine-day memorial, a whole range of Ukrainian political activists that earlier showed us no sympathy, and even condemned our organization for this or that, openly declared their recognition of UNA-UNSO.'[20] The deputy leader of the leading national democratic party Rukh, Tsymbalyuk, confirmed that this is more than wishful thinking by UNA-UNSO, stating that although it might not be sanctioned by the ministry of justice, UNA-UNSO was on 18 July sanctioned by the Ukrainian people.[21]

Fifth, as with the trade unions, UNA-UNSO has tried to gain a position as guardian of the Ukrainian Orthodox Church of the Kiev Patriarchate, which is independent of Moscow. In June 1992 the Ukrainian Orthodox Church split in two over the question of relations with Moscow. Led by the Metropolitan Filaret, those not recognizing Moscow's supremacy formed the Ukrainian Orthodox Church of the Kiev Patriarchate (UOCK). Those refusing to break with Moscow remained in the old Ukrainian Orthodox Church. During the split UNSO provided Filaret with bodyguards, who later caused a major scandal when, in the famous monastery Kiev Pecherska Lavra, they attacked the envoy sent by Moscow to lead the loyal branch of the church. The July 1995 incident at the Sofia cathedral is the latest evidence of the UOCK–UNA-UNSO connection.

The Ukrainian Orthodox Church of the Kiev Patriarchate controls about 2,000 parishes,[22] largely concentrated in the Ternopilska, Ivano-Frankivska, Lvivska and Kievska *oblasts*. Though the Kiev Patriarchate is considerably smaller than the Moscow-orientated Ukrainian Orthodox Church (about 6,000 parishes),[23] UNA-UNSO is likely to increase its support in western Ukraine and in Kiev by acting as its protector.

UNA-UNSO is working on three levels to increase its influence on Ukrainian politics, aiming first to capitalize on economic and social depression and win support from the most deprived; second, to ingratiate itself with more politically influential organizations, such as the trade unions, the church, and the national democrats, in the hope of acquiring influence though them; and, third, to frighten politicians and the public with displays of paramilitary power. It has had some limited success, but both its numbers and its influence remain small, and it is probably more an annoyance than a real threat in Ukraine today. Although some factors point to an increasingly important role for UNA-UNSO, it is likely to remain just a Ukrainian political obscenity.

Social instability

Social instability has the potential to jeopardize the further democratization of Ukraine, threaten its territorial integrity or in some way disrupt Ukrainian–Russian relations. The last two points will be dealt with respectively in the chapters on ethnic mobilization and separatism, and on Ukrainian–Russian relations; here it is appropriate to consider the impact of social instability on further democratization.

The standard of living of the majority of Ukrainians has fallen dramatically since independence. In May 1996, 67 per cent of the respondents in a countrywide survey characterized their material situation as bad or very bad. The same percentage also thought that 'everything in Ukraine is going in the wrong direction'.[24] Dissatisfaction by itself is no threat to further democratization; however, if it is combined with a widespread belief that a non-democratic regime would turn things for the better, and/

or with popular willingness to resort to non-democratic means of political action, then it may lead to social instability threatening democratization.

In January 1995 the US International Foundation for Electoral Systems made a survey of attitudes to political and economic reform in Ukraine. According to one of the compilers, Stephen Nix, there is only a core group of 25–30 per cent who long for the good old days, most of them middle-aged and elderly women.[25] Those who disdain the new system do not, therefore, constitute any large proportion of the Ukrainian population.

In addition, both political practice and social surveys in Ukraine indicate little willingness on the part of the population to resort to unlawful or non-democratic ways of expressing their opinions and demands. Aside from the actions of UNA-UNSO described above, it is hard to find examples of such actions in Ukraine since independence. One exception is the Crimean Tatars, who will be examined in Chapter 3. A comprehensive all-Ukrainian social survey from 1993 generated the following figures for the population's support of unlawful means of protest: boycott decisions by state organs 15 per cent; illegal meetings and demonstrations 5.9 per cent; illegal strikes 4 per cent; occupation of buildings 2 per cent; formation of independent armed units 3.5 per cent.[26] The same survey also found that the willingness to resort to such actions had decreased since 1992, while the willingness to use lawful actions such as legal strikes had increased. A similar survey from 1996 confirmed that although general willingness to protest against worsened living conditions had increased since 1993, the willingness to resort to unlawful means of protest remained low.[27]

This does not mean that social problems do not influence politics in Ukraine. The strikes by the mineworkers in Donbas during summer 1993 were probably the main reason behind the decision to bring the date of parliamentary and presidential elections forward to summer 1994, and strikes in the Donbas mines are still a major political headache for the political leadership in Kiev. The strikes, however, do not threaten Ukrainian democracy.

Civil–military relations

In 1991 Ukraine had more than enough military personnel to create credible armed forces, but there was a clear deficit of civilian personnel with sufficient insight into military matters to make their own independent judgments on how to proceed with military reform. Still, Ukraine has been able to secure relatively good civilian control over its armed forces, and has largely avoided army involvement in politics.

During Kravchuk's tenure of the presidency, the professional military were on the whole in charge of their own affairs. Kravchuk in many ways himself served as the civilian–military link, by keeping in close contact with the upper military echelons. This policy made the president fairly popular in the armed forces, and the top levels of the military, led by defence minister Radetsky, openly campaigned for Kravchuk in the 1994 presidential elections. This is one of very few instances of military involvement in Ukrainian politics.

The second democratic presidential elections in July 1994 were of major importance for civil–military relations. The new president, Leonid Kuchma, duly undertook a major reshuffle in all government structures, as part of which he appointed Valery Shmarov, his long-time associate from the defence industry, to the position of defence minister. Shmarov's name first captured the headlines as leader of the Ukrainian delegation that on 14 January 1994 finalized the Trilateral Agreement between Ukraine, Russia and the USA on Ukrainian nuclear disarmament – a step that did not win him many supporters in pro-nuclear military circles.

The arrival of a civilian in the top position in the military bureaucracy inevitably aroused concerns and suspicions. Shmarov did not rush into radical solutions, but took time to familiarize himself with the immediate problems. In order to overcome the instinctive reluctance among the military elite to accept civilian insight into defence matters, he had to strike an acceptable and meaningful balance between civilian and professional military control over the armed forces. For this he needed to build up civilian expertise in military matters from scratch.

Squabbles and discontent

From August 1994 to July 1995 Valery Shmarov held two key positions in the government: defence minister, and deputy prime minister with responsibility for the military-industrial complex. This did not leave him much time to dig deep into military affairs. According to *Izvestiya*, Shmarov initially limited his ruling over the army to 'gathering the generals twice a week in his office in order to haul them over the coals'.[28] What particularly annoyed the warriors was the new minister's habit of meddling in such completely innocent affairs as young recruits giving a helping hand at the generals' *dachas*. What was even worse, when Shmarov started reshuffling in the ministry, he was irritatingly stingy in awarding the generals' stars. In 1994, only 12 colonels of the 42 recommended received promotion to general. Small wonder that many in the upper echelons of the army found it provoking and symptomatic that the minister had ordered the removal of the portraits of the 'glorious Ukrainian Hetmans' from the walls of the general staff's headquarters. (The Hetmans were elected military leaders in the semi-independent Ukrainian lands from about 1500 until the destruction of Zaporozhian Sich in 1775.) Voicing the general dissatisfaction, General Anatoly Lopata, then chief of the general staff, told a meeting of army instructors in December 1994: 'The civilian defence minister is incompetent in his work.'[29] His audience, however, may have had a different opinion: what mattered for the rank and file officers was that since Shmarov had become defence minister, their salaries had started to arrive on time.

Spheres of authority

The problem of setting the limits of civilian control over military affairs in Ukraine remains essentially unresolved. It has generated tensions on both sides, as the minister has intervened in professional military matters and the general staff has tended to pursue its own political agenda. At times, these tensions rose quite high. In March 1995 Admiral Bezkorovainy, commander of the Ukrainian navy, tendered his resignation. He was annoyed because Shmarov had demanded a 50 per cent cut in the crew of the frigate *Hetman Sahaydachny*, scheduled for a visit to the Middle East. Shmarov compromised on the issue in order to avoid the admiral's resignation. He was, however, equally annoyed himself when the general staff, behind his back, lobbied parliamentary factions on the issue of troop reductions.

After months of manoeuvring, the general staff arrived at the conclusion that it was losing rather than gaining from the lack of clear delineation of authority. In May 1995 General Lopata complained: 'Only one thing remains unclear to me: that is the absence of a law regulating the delineation of functions between the civilian minister and the distinctly military structure, above all the general staff'.[30] Several drafts of such legislation were presented to Shmarov, but none received his approval. Understandably, the minister was reluctant to rush ahead with such a delineation: considering that his own apparatus was not yet either sufficiently competent or sufficiently reliable, he could be forced to concede so much authority to the general staff as to render his control over the military merely symbolic.

Civilian expertise

When Shmarov arrived in the defence ministry in August 1994, he found only a handful of civilian experts, none of them in a position of any influence; nor was there an available reservoir from which he could draw qualified experts. This problem had been created years before, since all the Soviet 'think-tanks' dealing with security matters were concentrated in Moscow. Shmarov had to hand-pick all his civilian managers and give them the opportunity to educate themselves to the level where they could face the military professionals as equals. This took time; but, according to General Zhukov, chief of the military department of Kiev University, quite an able civilian team started to emerge in the defence ministry.[31] Shmarov cautiously downplayed the controversies with the generals, stating only that 'the military demonstrate a lot of conservatism on many issues'.[32]

Two important developments in the summer of 1995 testified to forthcoming significant reforms. First, in July Shmarov relinquished the position of deputy prime minister to concentrate exclusively on his responsibilities in the defence ministry. Second, President Kuchma decided in August to create the General Military Inspection as a 'specialized presidential body of military control and expert analysis'.[33] Although chaired by General Hubenko, half of this fifty-strong Inspection would consist of civilian experts, and the military professionals who would make up the other half would work independently from the general staff. This presidential Inspection was expected to strengthen further the lines of civilian control over the army. However, the generals were not inclined to retreat from their positions without a fight.

Fighting the Hetmans

What made the struggle somewhat easier for Shmarov was that the Ukrainian generals – just like the Cossack Hetmans in the fifteenth to seventeenth centuries – found solidarity rather difficult. There was more to this than mere personal animosities: three regional groupings, from the Kiev, Odessa and Carpathian military districts, were competing for positions and influence.

General Radetsky – Shmarov's predecessor as defence minister – had brought to Kiev in late 1992 and early 1993 quite a number of his subordinates from the Odessa military district. This led to the team that ruled the military bureaucracy under Radetsky being nicknamed the 'Odessa Eleven'. In due course, Shmarov moved them one by one to secondary positions; General Kobzar, head of the Main Directorate for Education and Social-Psychological Work, was the last to go in February 1995, for 'misconduct in service'.[34] Presumably the main manifestation of this 'misconduct' was open support for Kuchma's rival, Kravchuk, in the July 1995 presidential elections. However, the influential 'clan' from the

Carpathian military district were disappointed in their expectation that now it was their turn to rule the army. Promotions were rather slow to come, and General Vasyl Sobkov, the Commander of the Ground Forces and former commander of the Carpathian military district, was in August 1995 reportedly actively working to remove Lopata and take over the position himself.[35] Shmarov seemed not to be taking sides, obviously preferring to keep the rivalries smouldering rather then to rely on one 'clan' and thus alienate the others.

Another sharp division in the Ukrainian officer corps runs along the line of nationalist ideology. In the army which Ukraine inherited from the USSR in early 1992, up to 90 per cent of senior officers and 70 per cent of general officers were non-Ukrainians, most of them Russians. That made the nationalist-minded politicians highly suspicious about the reliability of the armed forces; and indeed, unofficial surveys confirmed that the majority of officers would not fight in a conflict if the enemy was Russia.[36] The task of building a genuine 'patriotism' was entrusted to the first Ukrainian defence minister, General Morozov. Though an ethnic Russian himself, Morozov took a hard-nosed nationalistic line, making membership in the radicalized Union of Ukrainian Officers (UUO) a precondition of any promotion. The prestige of the UUO, however, now seems to be dwindling. This is essentially because the organization gives insufficient attention to the immense social problems of servicemen, and because most officers no longer feel that Ukraine's independence is seriously threatened.

Discontinuing the patriotic line, Shmarov insisted on a depoliticization of the army, and made professional capability the main criterion for evaluating officers. Still, he was careful not to offer the nationalists any serious provocation, and of six colonels promoted to general rank in 1995 five were ethnic Ukrainians. That was obviously not good enough for the marginalized UUO, but when it attempted to organize an officers' rally in mid-July 1995, its grave accusations against the defence minister failed to attract more than a few dozen listeners.

Gradually, the main bone of contention became the pace of army reform. Shmarov wanted to speed up reforms, in particular to reduce the number of troops and amount of hardware to keep in step with international arms control agreements. The upper echelons of the military, led by chief of the general staff Lopata and supported by deputies from the national-democratic camp, wanted instead to slow down the pace of reform and to concentrate on the army's social problems and on the need to maintain a viable defence industry. The conflict became intolerable, and President Kuchma removed Lopata from his position in February 1996. A month later Kuchma surprisingly appointed a young lieutenant-general, Aleksandr Zatynaiko (49), as new chief of the general staff.

Shmarov left his position in July 1996, as part of the government reshuffle after the adoption of the new Ukrainian constitution, and after heavy criticism from (among others) the secretary of the Security Council, Volodymyr Horbulin. Horbulin called Shmarov an 'undisciplined person', held him partly responsible for the bad financial situation of the armed forces, and criticized him for not regulating the delineation of functions between the minister and the general staff.[37] On 11 July 1996 President Kuchma appointed as his new defence minister Lieutenant-General Aleksandr Kuzmyk. The new defence minister is only 42 years old, and is yet another example of Kuchma bypassing the upper layer of generals when making appointments to the top positions in the defence ministry. One reason for the appointment of officers from the lower ranks may be an expectation that such men, grateful for early promotion, would probably be more loyal and accommodating towards the civilian leadership than those from the independent-minded top layer.

The armed forces have shown little interest in participating in politics. But, the 'battle with the Hetmans' is not over. There is still some way to go before the armed forces are solidly under civilian control. However, the prospects are clearly enhanced by internal disunity in the military high command and, as Richard Woff has put it, the lack of 'the political clout still enjoyed by the post-Soviet Russian military establishment'.[38] Relatively stable civilian control over the armed forces already makes Ukraine much more confident about its near future than Russia, where the army remains an independent and highly unpredictable political actor.

Summary

In evaluating the consolidation of Ukrainian democracy I have chosen to borrow the concepts of attitudinal behavioural and constitutional features developed by Juan J. Linz and Alfred Stepan. According to them, 'attitudinally, democracy becomes the only game in town when, even in the face of severe political and economic crisis, the overwhelming majority of the people believe that any further political change must emerge from within the parameters of democratic procedure'.[39] There is no doubt about the severity of the political and economic crisis in Ukraine; nevertheless, 74.8 per cent of the population voted in the first round and 65 per cent in the second round of the March–April 1994 parliamentary

23

elections.[40] According to a June 1996 survey, only 25 per cent of the respondents could accept that democratic norms such as free speech or the right to form political parties could be limited in the name of 'state interests'.[41] As we have seen, a plethora of political parties has grown up in Ukraine. The overwhelming majority of people do not seem to have turned away from democracy, despite harsh living conditions.

The next test, according to Linz and Stepan, is that, behaviourally, 'democracy becomes the only game in town when no significant political group seriously attempts to overthrow the democratic regime or to promote domestic or international violence in order to secede from the state'.[42] As we have seen from the discussion on the UNA-UNSO and on civil–military relations, the organization that is willing to attempt overthrow is not able to do so, and the organization that might be able to attempt overthrow is not willing. As we shall see later, there are separatist tendencies in Ukraine, especially in Crimea, but they have so far not made use of domestic or international violence to achieve their goals.

The third and last test, according to Linz and Stepan, is that, constitutionally, 'democracy becomes the only game in town when all of the actors in the polity become habituated to the fact that political conflict within the state will be resolved according to established norms, and that violations of these norms are likely to be both ineffective and costly'.[43] Both the Kravchuk and the Kuchma administrations have been accused, probably not without reason, of using state media to their advantage. Both administrations have also established state organs – Kravchuk with his State Council and Kuchma with his strong presidential administration – whose authority was not warranted by existing legislation. However, Kravchuk readily gave up power when he lost to Kuchma in the presidential elections. Both gave in to or compromised with the parliament when accused of not following the rules. The major problem was that, in the absence of a constitution, the rules were uncertain. That problem has been rectified by the adoption on 28 June 1996 of the new constitution.

Thus, although few would yet call Ukraine a fully-fledged democracy, most indicators point to it moving decisively in that direction.

Chapter 3

Ethnic mobilization and separatism

In the spring of 1994 the US Central Intelligence Agency (CIA), in a widely cited report, presented one of the most pessimistic scenarios yet advanced for independent Ukraine. The report's main conclusion was that a splintering of Ukraine along the Dniepr River could be imminent. The Ukrainian presidential elections in July 1994, in which the citizens west of the Dniepr voted for Kravchuk and those to the east for Kuchma, were taken as yet further confirmation of the ongoing disintegration of Ukraine. Nevertheless, in June 1995 Kuchma stated: 'There is no longer any danger of Ukraine splitting up the way Yugoslavia did. I am the president, I should know.'[1]

This chapter aims to explain why President Kuchma felt able confidently to brush aside prophecies of Ukrainian disintegration along ethnic lines, discounting violent conflict between a Ukrainian-dominated western part and a Russian-dominated eastern part.[2] The first part of the chapter discusses eastern and southern Ukraine* (ESU), and the second part focuses on Crimea.

A. EASTERN AND SOUTHERN UKRAINE

Sociologist Rogers Brubaker asserts that the likelihood of minority ethnic communities mobilizing for either separatist or strong regionalist demands depends upon the interplay among three 'fields of differentiated and competing positions': the minority itself, the nationalizing state of residence, and the historical homeland.[3] In Ukraine these fields are,

---

*By eastern and southern Ukraine I mean the *oblasts* Kharkivska, Luhanska, Donetska, Dnipropetrovska, Zaporizhzhska, Khersonska, Mykolayivska and Odeska.

respectively, the Russian minority, the Ukrainian nationalizing state and the Russian Federation. The label 'field' is used to emphasize that each entity is an arena for competing ideas rather than a uniform actor. Ukrainian independence, for example, is conceived of in many different ways among the Russian minority in Ukraine. What matters is which conception is the prevailing one. A conception can prevail either because a majority of the community in each field holds it, or because it is held by a majority of the most influential members of the community.

Ethnic groups have different ambitions regarding their mobilization. The most important distinction is between separatism – meaning a change of state borders – and some degree of autonomy. Separatism clearly bears the greatest potential for conflict, since the scope for compromise is very small. However, demands for autonomy can also cause conflict, both because autonomy is often considered the first step towards separatism, and because separatism can serve the purposes of those whose real aim is autonomy. References to the disintegration of Ukraine therefore here include attempts both at separating off parts of the country and at achieving a degree of autonomy unacceptable to Ukrainian central authorities.

The Russian minority and Ukrainian independence

In 1991 more than 90 per cent of the population in Ukraine voted for independence from the Soviet Union; in Russian-dominated ESU, more than 80 per cent did so.[4] According to analysts, this was more because of an expectation that Ukraine would be better off economically than Russia than because voters had any strong feeling for the 'Ukrainian cause'. This economic expectation was not fulfilled. Today living conditions may even be slightly better in Russia than in Ukraine. That, at least, is what 59 per cent of Ukrainians believed in 1995.[5] The introduction of Ukrainian as the only official language of the country, and of state symbols and teaching of history alien to most Russians, the refusal so far to organize Ukraine as a federation or to participate fully in cooperation within the CIS, troubled Ukrainian–Russian relations, the economic crisis – all this has seriously alienated large parts of the population in ESU from the idea of independence. In an opinion poll in ESU in the spring of 1994, only 24 per cent of the respondents said they would vote for independence if the referendum were repeated today,[6] and in a March 1996 survey one-third of respondents in ESU called for full reintegration of Ukraine with the other former Soviet republics.[7]

The history of separatism in eastern and southern Ukraine

There are four main political forces in eastern and southern Ukraine: the Communist Party, the trade unions, the moderate parties and the separatist parties. Initially the central authorities in Kiev feared that not only the separatists, but also the Communists and the trade unions, would voice separatist demands. Until now they have not done so.

The Communists advocate some kind of a restored union of Soviet states, and do not see border changes as a means to achieve this goal. Moreover, the Communist Party of Ukraine, despite its dominance in the east and south, is an all-Ukrainian organization. The need to accommodate pro-independence sentiments in western and central Ukraine within the Communist Party was clearly demonstrated at the party's congress in Kiev on 11 and 12 March 1995. Despite some sulking by eastern and southern Communists, it was decided that the Communist Party of Ukraine's goal is a union of *sovereign* sister nations.

The trade unions – both the former official unions that still organize the majority of Ukrainian workers and the new 'independent' trade unions – have been careful not to let their protest actions provide opportunities for the voicing of separatist demands. Though there are both personal and ideological ties between them and the regionalists, the trade unionists have rejected attempts to use their strikes in a campaign for autonomy for the Donbas (Donetska and Luhanska *oblasts*). At one of its meetings during the June/July 1993 strikes, the central coordination committee for the strikes decided to 'remove from the lists of demands any questions concerning autonomy for Donbas in any form, as this might lead to discord in society and damage the unity of Ukraine'.[8] Or, as one of the leaders of the Independent Miners' Union said in October 1994: 'Please tell me what idiot would be against his own independence.'[9]

The moderates are largely represented by the Labour Party of Ukraine and the Liberal Party of Ukraine. Both are all-Ukrainian parties that originated in eastern Ukraine. The Labour Party – nicknamed 'the party of red directors' – advocates gradual economic reform with maximum concern for the interests of large state enterprises, whereas the Liberal Party wants rapid and radical economic reform. In this context, however, the main point is that they both support Ukrainian independence.

Those not ready to accept Ukrainian independence face one very serious dilemma. If they demand either total independence or unification with Russia for ESU, this will automatically imply a recognition of the independence of the rest of Ukraine. Most elements in ESU opposed to

Ukrainian independence are not ready to accept this, and have therefore chosen the reintegration option instead of the separatist one. This is a crucial difference between ESU and Crimea. However, the anti-independence forces are at the same time eager to accentuate the historically non-Ukrainian character of ESU (especially the Donbas).[10] If, therefore, they have to abandon their hope of reunification, or they perceive that popular feeling is increasing in favour of separatism, a switch from the reunification line to the separatist line can easily be contrived. After all, Crimea has already set the example.

There are two main parties working against Ukrainian independence: the Civic Congress of Ukraine (CCU) and the Slavic Unity Party (SUP). As early as December 1990 the first regional movement, the Inter-movement of Donbas, was founded in eastern Ukraine in reaction to the 1989 Ukrainian Language Law that made Ukrainian the official state language. Several similar movements were formed after Ukraine became independent, and in June 1992 most of them joined forces to establish the CCU. These events all took place in the city of Donetsk, which became the centre of regionalists in ESU. In September 1991 a committee was even set up by the Donetska *oblast* council to organize a referendum on the re-establishment of the short-lived 1918 Krivorozhsko–Donetsk republic. Kiev feared for some time that Donetsk and Donbas would come to pose a serious threat to the territorial integrity and maybe even the independence of Ukraine. That development did not take place. The only strong organized popular movements in Donbas are the trade unions, and they have continued their policy of not mixing trade union activity with reintegration, regionalist or separatist demands. As for the political elite in Donbas, it is concentrating its efforts on securing for itself as many positions of power as possible in Kiev. Since Kuchma became president the Donbas elite's main rival has been the Dnipropetrovsk elite, who by summer 1996 seemed to have won a preliminary victory.[11]

Despite considerable popular support for the reunification ideas of the CCU in ESU,[12] this support has not resulted in any visible increase in the popularity of the Congress itself. Only two members of the Civic Congress (Yuriy Boldyrev from Donetsk and Vladimir Alekseev from Kharkov) were elected to the Ukrainian parliament during the several rounds of parliamentary elections in 1994. In the regional elections, none of the ESU regional leaders, or 'governors' as they are often called, came from the Civic Congress.

Representatives of the CCU and SUP, together with anti-independence activists from the Communist Party, the Socialist Party and the Kharkov-based Pro-Union Committee, have established what is called the Kharkov

Council. A press release from the Council's meeting at the end of June 1995 reads: 'We are opposed to forcible unification of Ukraine's different regions as well as to its artificial division. Our goal is a Ukraine in a restored union.'[13] The CCU is cooperating with Ukrainian left-wing forces, though this line is disputed internally. The SUP is clearly non-communist, and has even flirted with UNA-UNSO and its idea of a Slavic empire centred in Kiev. However, after the SUP's third congress in Kharkov in May 1996, this flirtation seemed to be over. The congress ended with a major street brawl between UNA-UNSO activists and the SUP's Russian guests, who had difficulty accepting that Moscow would be subordinated to Kiev in the future unitary Slavic state.[14]

Besides numerous conferences and calls in the press for reunification, the most concrete action so far taken by the anti-independence forces is the less then wholly successful January 1995 collection of signatures to a proposal for an economic, military and economic reunification of Russia, Belarus, Kazakstan and Ukraine.

Although voices advocating the establishment of an independent Novorossiya republic were heard in southern Ukraine as early as 1990,[15] and nationally minded Ukrainians were offended by the spring 1995 decision to raise a statue of Catherine II in Odessa (many Ukrainians consider her responsible for the decline of Ukrainian autonomy in the second part of the eighteenth century), little or no organized anti-independence political activity exists in southern Ukraine. Organized political life is generally less active here than in eastern Ukraine. There are, according to one observer, almost no political parties in Odessa. Though anti-Kiev terminology, according to the same observer, is quite popular among Odessa politicians, their demands amount to no more than the establishment of a free economic zone.[16]

In summary, since Ukraine became independent in 1991, attempts at mobilization against its independence in ESU have been few and scattered. Opposition was voiced primarily by the two anti-independence parties, the CCU and the SUP. These parties, together with anti-independence-minded Communists and Socialists, organized meetings, petitions and other activities for the restoration of the old Union. Public support both for these parties and for their activities was very limited. The anti-independence groups made the crucial strategic decision to demand reunification rather then separation. The situation in eastern and southern Ukraine therefore differed from that in Crimea in two ways: public support for anti-independence movements was much smaller, and the demand was for reunification, not for separation.

29

Accounting for the non-mobilization of the Russian minority

In accounting for the non-mobilization of Russians in ESU, I will focus on four distinguishing characteristics of this ethnic minority: perceptive, emotional, structural and deliberative/rational.[17] Perceptive characteristics refer to how the Russian minority conceive of Ukrainian independence and their own minority position. Emotional characteristics refer to the degree of ethnic comfort the Russians feel in Ukraine, in relation both to the majority Ukrainian population and to Ukrainian authorities. Structural characteristics refer to the positions the Russian minority occupy in political and economic life in Ukraine. Deliberative/rational characteristics refer to the difference between what the Russian minority might think, feel and desire, and what they realistically think is possible and worthwhile mobilizing for – that is, cost-benefit analysis on a popular scale.

Perceptive characteristics

The Russian diasporas can be described in terms of two dimensions: *self-defined ethnic identity* and *political loyalty*.[18] On each dimension it is possible to distinguish the three positions: *historic fatherland* (Russia), *state of residence* (Ukraine) and *other* (Soviet or regional).

One indicator of the most popular self-defined ethnic identity in the ESU public is an opinion poll conducted among citizens of Donetsk in March 1994. Asked whether they considered their identity to be Ukrainian, Russian or Soviet, 45.4 per cent answered Soviet, 25.9 per cent Russian, and 22.2 per cent Ukrainian. This means that a total of 70 per cent of the inhabitants of Donetsk had a self-defined ethnic identity that was not Ukrainian. Further, the tendency to identify as Soviet was almost equal for Russians and Ukrainians (by passport): respectively 50.0 per cent and 45.5 per cent.[19]

The problem for the 45.4 per cent who feel Soviet is, of course, that the state with which they identify has disappeared. This means that a large section of the population of ESU can be expected to redefine their self-defined ethnic identity in the years to come. The hitherto fairly limited extent of this re-identification has probably restrained ethnic mobilization in ESU. However, when the process does get under way, it is likely to have consequences for the potential of ethnic mobilization. Which way or ways the process is likely to go is hard to say. Ukrainian political scientist Dmytro Vydrin points out that considerable numbers of Russian-speaking Ukrainians are carrying 'a hidden complex of guilt towards Ukraine' because they use the 'grand and mighty Russian language'.[20] If this is the case then at least some of those Soviet-identifying Russian speakers who are Ukrainian by passport can be expected to change to a Ukrainian self-defined ethnic identity.

Besides the Russian and Ukrainian self-defined ethnic identities, several observers have pointed out the possibility of a local one. While stressing that Donbas is beyond doubt Russian, Dmitry Kornilov, ideological leader of the Civic Congress, also emphasizes that 'ethnic Russians in Ukraine are not at all identical to Russians in Russia.'[21] Moreover, many Russianized Ukrainians of ESU might find such a local self-defined ethnic identity closer to their heart than a Ukrainian one. To what extent it can be found in ESU has not yet been examined, but it probably remains an option.

The more Russian the prevalent public self-defined ethnic identity becomes, the more one might also expect an extended political loyalty towards the historical homeland of Russia, and consequently an increase in the potential for separatism. Correspondingly, the more a Ukrainian self-defined ethnic identity exists, the less the potential for separatism will be. Finally, if a local self-defined ethnic identity becomes prevalent, demands for autonomy can be expected to increase, but the potential for separatism will not necessarily increase. For the Ukrainian central authorities it will be easier to reach compromises with regionalists than with separatists.

Of equal, or even larger, importance are the self-defined ethnic identity and political loyalty that predominate in the ESU political and economic elite. Representatives of this group are regularly questioned about their attitude towards Ukrainian independence and the position of ESU in the interface between Russian and Ukrainian interests. Independently of whether they define themselves as Russians, Ukrainians, or 'locals', the great majority express political loyalty to Ukraine.[22] The percentage of Russians politically loyal to Ukraine is therefore probably larger in the ESU elite than in the ESU public.

There are various reasons for this stance. One cannot dismiss the fact that independence seems legitimate to many of them, but other, less altruistic reasons may also be present. First, it is easier for the ESU elite to influence decisions if they are made in Kiev rather than in Moscow. Simultaneously, independence makes it easier for elites to attain the highest political posts in the state, since there are fewer competitors. This is probably where the perceptions of the elite differ most markedly from popular perceptions in ESU. Whereas at the popular level there is a widespread feeling of losing economically by independence, quite the opposite is true at the elite level. The pay-off of independence is therefore perceived in different ways at the elite and at the popular level. Since ESU is both the demographic and the economic centre of gravity in Ukraine, these areas are for the foreseeable future likely to have a strong say in Kiev. There is also a strong fear that attempts at reunification or separatism will provoke serious conflicts in society, possibly even bloodshed. Such a turn of events would be bad for business and dangerous for everybody. Finally, it is also likely that the strong linkage between anti-independence rhetoric and communist nostalgia is fostering the ESU political and economic elite's allegiance towards Ukraine. So far there is no significant organized anti-independence pro-reform alternative in ESU.

The support among the ESU political and economic elite for Ukrainian independence is fortifying Ukrainian territorial unity not only because these people are influential by virtue of their position as decision-makers, but also because they provide an alternative as advocates of Ukrainian independence to the largely western Ukrainian national democrats who are regarded with strong suspicion in ESU. The ESU elite is therefore much more likely to promote pro-Ukrainian sentiments in the ESU population than are envoys of Rukh or the URP.

Therefore, although an increase in political loyalty for the historical homeland, expressed through the wish for Ukrainian–Russian unity, is clearly taking place among the ESU public, those who express these sympathies still account for only about half of the ESU population, and they are very sparsely represented among the political and economic elite.

Emotional characteristics
The ethnic comfort of Russians in ESU has to be measured on two levels: among the ESU public and towards central Ukrainian authorities.

Russian citizens in general feel comfortable in ESU and have few complaints about the Ukrainians among whom they live. Russians are not very different from Ukrainians. The differences between their languages can be compared to the differences between Norwegian and Swedish. Except for the Uniates* in western Ukraine, they also share a common religion. In addition to the social similarities between the two nations, the ethnic boundary is also blurred. It is difficult to know how many of the

---

* The Uniate church is an independent church in western Ukraine that accepts the religious superiority of the Pope, while retaining the Orthodox rituals. Established as a compromise between Polish church authorities and parts of the Ukrainian Orthodox clergy in the Union of Brest in 1596, the Uniate church has about 3 million believers in Ukraine today.

Russian-speaking Ukrainians feel more Russian than Ukrainian. As a general rule, the further west one goes, the stronger the Ukrainian identity is, but any clear line of demarcation is impossible to draw. Many ESU Ukrainians probably have more in common with the Russians among whom they live than with the Ukrainians of western Ukraine. Though one can undoubtedly find cultural differences between Ukrainians and Russians, there are few examples of political conflicts resulting from purely cultural differences. Moreover, although there is a history of political conflict between Russia and Ukraine, there is little or no history of ethnic conflict between Russians and Ukrainians in Ukraine.

It is difficult to predict future relations for coexisting national groups with small cultural differences. According to John Coakley, the general trend is that 'the more adjacent the minority is to its host society, the less the probability of mutual mistrust, other things being equal'.[23] This is not always the case: if the minority feels a strong need to distance itself from others, those closest might be the prime targets, since they are the ones from whom it is most difficult to achieve distance. Vojislav Stankovcic talks of the 'complex of small differences' exemplified by the Serbs and the Croats.[24]

How, then, do Russians and Ukrainians in Ukraine view each other? In early 1992 the University of Maryland, in cooperation with social scientists in Russia and Ukraine, conducted a survey on ethnic attitudes among Russians and Ukrainians in Russia and in Ukraine.[25] The respondents were all high-school students aged 16 and 17. Though one cannot assume that the results are valid for the entire population, they do give an indication of Russians' and Ukrainians' attitudes towards one another in Ukraine. Asked whether they liked Ukrainians, 77 per cent of Russians in Ukraine said that they either 'liked' or 'liked very much' Ukrainians. Similarly, 70 per cent of Ukrainians said they 'liked' or 'liked very much' Russians. Another large sociological survey from spring 1993 confirms these results, finding that only 11.1 per cent of Russians in Ukraine think that ethnic conflicts are possible in Ukraine, 38 per cent that the relations between nationalities are better in Ukraine than they are in Russia, and only 12.8 per cent that they are worse.[26] The conclusion must therefore be that the Russians in ESU and Ukrainians generally get along quite well. The 'complex of small differences' does not seem to be present to any significant extent in the population of Ukraine.

There are, however, problems in the relationship between the Russian minority and the Ukrainian central authorities. A majority of Russians want a higher legal status for the Russian language, and the opportunity to have both Russian and Ukrainian citizenship. In opinion polls held simultaneously with the Ukrainian parliamentary elections in March 1994, voters of Donetska and Luhanska *oblasts* were asked whether they wanted the Ukrainian constitution to make Russian the second state language. In Donetska 87.1 per cent and in Luhanska 79.9 per cent said yes.[27]

In western Ukraine, the Congress of Russian Communities of Ukraine's Western Oblasts was established in autumn 1994 to protect the interests of the Russian community. According to one of the organizers, the three years of Ukrainian independence have been the 'most terrible for the local Russians,' and he even accused the authorities of the Lvivska, Ivano-Frankivska and Ternopilska *oblasts* of conducting 'ethnic cleansing'.[28] Though it is reasonable to assume that pressure might be higher on the Russians in nationalistic western Ukraine, this pressure has been insufficient either to provoke significant mobilization of the Russian population there or to create any tangible concern for their fate among their fellow ethnic Russians in ESU.

Structural characteristics
The structural characteristics of the Russian minority in Ukraine are best described at three different levels: the individual, the regional and the international.

(1) The individual level: Russians versus Ukrainians Ethnic mobilization is often instigated in instances where members of one ethnic group are excluded from career opportunities in economic or political life because of their ethnicity. Such exclusion is relatively rare in Ukraine. The only real limitation is on higher positions in politics or the civil service where there is a demand for knowledge of the Ukrainian language. For example, President Kuchma had to brush up his Ukrainian after being elected president. This makes it harder for Russians than for Ukrainians to achieve certain positions. However, if Russians applying for these positions are willing to learn Ukrainian (which, given the two languages' proximity is not very difficult), their ethnic background is not likely to hold them back. For example, Ukraine's first minister of defence, Konstantin Morozov, was an ethnic Russian. According to the former Ukrainian presidential adviser Dmytro Vydrin, ethnic Russians occupy more than 20 per cent of the higher offices in Ukrainian politics and the civil service.[29] This number corresponds quite closely with their percentage of the population.

(2) The regional level: Russian-dominated versus Ukrainian-dominated regions There are more systemic differences at the regional level than at the individual level. First, there is a widespread belief in ESU that it is subsidizing the poorer regions of western and central Ukraine – a belief that is confirmed by official Ukrainian financial statistics. Most western and southern *oblasts* get to keep a larger percentage of the taxes collected locally and are more heavily subsidized by the state budget than are their eastern and central counterparts. The ESU *oblasts* Zaporizhzhska, Donetska, Dnipropetrovska, Poltavska, Sumska and Kiev are major contributors to the federal budget.[30] This redistribution of wealth is one of the main reasons behind the demands for regional economic autonomy. The anti-independence forces make extensive use of this argument. They claim that the western Ukrainian nationalists tore Ukraine away from Russia, but since they were unable to feed themselves they also took eastern Ukraine with them to have something to feed on. Because of the indisputably redistributive character of the Ukrainian state budget, such arguments are persuasive in ESU. Economic autonomy is therefore a demand voiced by practically every political force in ESU, except the tiny local divisions of the national-democratic parties. However, most politicians emphasize that demands for economic autonomy are not a cover for demands endangering Ukrainian independence and territorial integrity.[31]

Second, there is a certain degree of cultural division of labour in Ukraine. Russian-dominated eastern Ukraine has 45 per cent of Ukrainian industry but only 34 per cent of the population.[32] Mass lay-offs in industry are an expected consequence of economic reform, and a main worry in Kiev has been that Russians would be harder hit than Ukrainians. This could spark ethnic mobilization of the Russian minority against Ukrainian independence.

Since 1991, many observers have singled out ESU as the economically least promising region in Ukraine. The *Economist*'s correspondent in Kiev in 1993 described the situation of the Russian minority in ESU in the following way: 'A majority work in the rust belt of Eastern Ukraine, which has no economic future. Thus ethnic Russians live in the areas that will bear the brunt of the economic slump.'[33] It is true that important ESU sectors such as the coal industry are totally dependent on state subsidies. But it is not at all certain that the economic future of Russian-dominated ESU is as grim as the *Economist*'s correspondent concluded; and, most importantly, its prospects are not necessarily any worse than those of the rest of Ukraine. The problems of the coal industry, for example, have as much to do with lack of investment and modernization in the mines over the past 20 years as with the lack of mineral deposits. *Financial Times* correspondent Matthew Kaminski, in an optimistic article, wrote: 'It is estimated that a quarter of Ukraine's economic potential lies with the Donbas's steel mills, coal pits, farms, sea ports, factories and coal, manganese and iron deposits.'[34] Also, despite the lack of economic reform under Kravchuk, an entrepreneurial spirit has sprung up in Donbas at least as much as in other regions of Ukraine. The summer 1994 local elections in ESU brought a considerable number of reform-minded politicians into government in city and *oblast* councils. This was in quite striking contrast to the parliamentary elections, where ESU voters gravitated towards anti-reform left-wingers. Both the resources and the people needed for economic progress in the future, therefore, seem to be present to no smaller extent in ESU than in other parts of Ukraine.

Third, a phenomenon which for some time gave impetus to demands for greater independence for ESU, and which could do so again in the future, is unbalanced recruitment to the central political elite in Kiev. After 1991 many national democrats came into leading positions in Kiev as a result of the nomenklatura–national democrat alliance. Most of these were from western or central Ukraine. This gave rise to a feeling in ESU that the central government was occupied exclusively by nationalistic westerners. The miners' strikes of June 1993 were partially a response to this development. Hryhori Nemyria, Professor of Political Science at Donetsk University, explained the strikes as 'Eastern Ukraine's political revenge. After many years of the recruitment of Ukraine's political elites from the Donbas, it is Western Ukraine which now is prominent. The current strike is an effort to turn the tables back again.'[35] The dominance of western and central Ukrainians in Kiev changed, however, when Kuchma became president. Today the question discussed is whether it is the Kiev clan, the Dnipropetrovsk clan or the Donetsk clan that has the most say in Kiev.

(3) The international level: Russians in Ukraine versus Russians in Russia Kiev's main worry in this respect is that economic reform may fail in Ukraine at the same time as it succeeds in Russia. If Russians in Russia have a better standard of living than those across the border in Ukraine, the potential for separatism will increase. Former Ukrainian presidential adviser Dmytro Vydrin considers this to be the only factor that could spark a strong separatist movement in the Russian minority in ESU.[36] Were economic reform to fail in Ukraine while succeeding in Russia, the consequences might be serious both for political stability in Ukraine and for

Russian–Ukrainian relations.

On the other hand, developments in Russia may also reduce that country's attractiveness to the Russians of ESU. The war in Chechenia is an obvious example. Parents in the Russian Rostov *oblast,* which borders on the ESU, started to buy flats in the Ukrainian Luhanska *oblast* for their sons after this war began. This enables the young men to register in Ukraine, thus avoiding the Russian military draft.[37] Such developments are likely to have an impact on the Russian minority of ESU.

Deliberative/rational characteristics

The characteristics noted above describe features of the Russian minority in Ukraine that make demands for autonomy or even separatism more or less likely. What these approaches do not take sufficiently into account, however, is the importance of rational calculating processes on a massive scale. While they address reasons why the Russian minority of Ukraine would want or not want to separate from Ukraine, they do not address the cost-benefit thinking of many Russians after their initial clarification of preferences regarding autonomy and separatism. Each individual, when taking a stance on the idea of separatism, is also likely to ask how much the accomplishment of separation from Ukraine is going to cost, and what undesirable side-effects it is likely to yield. At least three such rationalizing processes seem present on a mass scale in ESU.

First, a splintering of Ukraine is not likely to take place without bloodshed. The western and central Ukrainians are not going to let ESU go without a fight, and under any circumstances it would be very difficult to decide where to draw the border. It is likely that these facts are recognized by large sections of the Russian minority, and that they judge it better to accept Ukrainian independence, which they may not want but can tolerate, than risk civil war. Several bloody attempts at separatism in the post-Soviet area – for example Nagorno-Karabakh or Chechenia – have probably had a sobering effect on the Russian minority in this respect.

Second, despite some nostalgia for the past, the majority of the population do not want the Soviet system back.[38] Since the anti-independence and the anti-reform movements have so far run in harness, supporting the anti-independence activists would automatically also mean supporting the revival of the Soviet system with its failed planned economy. The separatist and ardently Communist leadership in the breakaway Pridnyestrovya republic in Moldova is a case in point. Relapse into communism could therefore be an undesirable side-effect of supporting some of the existing separatist organizations.

Third, since independence there has probably been a widespread feeling in ESU that some kind of a reunification of the former Soviet republics is bound to take place. The establishment of the CIS, other reintegrating efforts such as the extensive cooperation treaty between Russia and Belarus, or treaties for wide-ranging security cooperation and military bases in Armenia and Georgia, as well as Ukraine's economic dependence upon Russia, have provided a basis for such presumptions. There is not much sense in putting political stability in Ukraine at risk by promulgating separatist slogans if some kind of a reunification is likely in the relatively near future anyway.

The nationalizing Ukrainian state and its Russian minority

The nationalizing (for which read 'nation-building') Ukrainian state has treated its Russian minority relatively well since independence. Evidence for this is supplied by studies of the formal and informal methods of accommodation applied by the state, by polls of the ethnic comfort of Russians in Ukraine, and by statements from international observers studying the conditions of ethnic minorities in Ukraine. One observer, James Gow, goes so far as to say: 'The importance of internal politics for stability and security has been exemplified in Ukraine's practice *vis-à-vis* minorities ... Ukrainian security practice offers elements of a model for post-communist societies.'[39]

Two kinds of legal rights are particularly central to ethnic minorities: equality of citizenship and cultural rights. The question of citizenship in Ukraine is regulated through the Law on Citizenship, adopted by the parliament in October 1991. The law incorporated a version of the so-called zero option, whereby persons permanently resident in Ukraine for more than five years, at the time of the adoption of the law, became Ukrainian citizens. Though the draft law initially contained no provision for dual citizenship, this possibility was inserted into the legislation after a heated debate in parliament.[40] Dual citizenship was, however, made dependent upon conclusion of agreements on this issue with other states. Despite strong pressure from Russia, no such agreements have so far been made.

The fundamental cultural right Russians in Ukraine have demanded is for recognition of their language. The Ukrainian law on languages adopted by the parliament in October 1989 gave priority to, and promoted the use of, Ukrainian,[41] but also repeatedly stated that all nationalities in Ukraine have a right to use their own languages. In addition to the language law, the law on national minorities in Ukraine adopted on 25 June

1992 further confirmed the rights of national minorities in linguistic, cultural and religious affairs.[42] A 1995 census also shows that the rights of the Russian language are not merely acknowledged on paper. At the beginning of 1995, for example, 42.7 per cent of Ukrainian children were studying in Russian-language schools, and Russian-language programmes occupied two-thirds of total television broadcasting time (not including ORT 1, the official channel of the Russian Federation).[43]

The Russian language, therefore, appears to enjoy considerable rights both on paper and in practice. It has not, however, been granted status as a second state language. That position was confirmed by the adoption in June 1996 of the Ukrainian constitution, which says that Ukrainian is the only state language of Ukraine – despite the fact that most surveys show that between 40 and 50 per cent of the population consider Russian to be their first language. The raising of the status of Russian to that of a second state language, and the introduction of the option of dual citizenship, are demands that enjoy considerable support among a majority of Russians in Ukraine.

The Russian minority in Ukraine is therefore not entirely satisfied with its citizenship and cultural rights, but the level of dissatisfaction is not high enough to spark ethnic mobilization.

Ukraine's liberal policy towards its Russian minority

The adoption by the Ukrainian government of a liberal policy towards the Russian minority in Ukraine can be analysed in the light of rational, structural and ideological factors.

Rational factors

The Russian minority's size and its demographic trends are the two primary rational factors affecting Ukraine's liberal policy towards its ethnic Russians.

The size of the Russian population – 11.4 million – makes it politically dangerous to ignore its demands, especially since many Russified Ukrainians are likely to share most of the Russian minority's political sentiments. At the same time, the Russian population is sufficiently small not to create a fear that it will dominate political life, a cause of concern in some Baltic states.

The relative demographic trends of the minority and majority populations are interesting because in many countries the majority feels threatened by a steady increase in the percentage of the minority. There

39

has been a steady increase in the percentage of Russians in Ukraine: in 1959 Ukrainians constituted 77 per cent of the population, but in 1989 this figure had fallen to 72.7 per cent, while the percentage of Russians rose in the same period from 17 per cent to 22.1 per cent.[44] Immigration of Russians and outmigration of Ukrainians is part of the explanation, but even more important is the slow process of 'reidentification' that took place during the Soviet period. Children with parents of different nationalities, one of whom was Russian, in a majority of cases chose Russian as their own nationality. If this process should continue in independent Ukraine, the Ukrainian authorities could adopt a definite aim of halting the rising percentage of Russians in the population. However, it would then be easier and safer to encourage the forging of a national identity among the ethnic Ukrainians, so that they do not reidentify, rather than to try to turn Russians into Ukrainians.

Structural factors
Because of international norms and pressures, states do not normally have a free hand in the treatment of their minorities. In the Ukrainian case it is necessary to distinguish between the limits imposed by Russian demands and the limits imposed by the norms of the international community. The pressure felt in Kiev is based both on the fear of how the authorities in the Kremlin would react to maltreatment of the Russians in Ukraine, and on the fear that these Russians could develop into some kind of 'fifth column' if maltreated, making interference by Russia even easier. For example, *Strategy for the Development of Ukraine*, a document prepared by the National Institute of Strategic Studies, discusses ways in which Russia might become a threat to Ukrainian security. It mentions 'inflaming anti-Ukrainian feelings among the ethnic Russians of Ukraine', creating 'an arc of instability ranging eastwards from the southern areas bordering Pridniestrovya through Crimea to the borders of the Don Cossacks'.[45]

A human rights discourse is influential in the international community today. Countries maltreating their national minorities are discredited. Ukraine, striving so hard to be accepted by the West, would lose much credibility if it did not treat its minorities well. It has signed several international agreements on human rights, and in July 1992 it confirmed its adherence to the UN International Covenant on Civil and Political Rights, by recognizing the competence of the UN Human Rights Committee. Since January 1992 it has been a member of the Organization for Security and Cooperation in Europe (OSCE; formerly CSCE). Together with the other OSCE member states, Ukraine acceded to the 1992 Helsinki Document, which among other things provided for a High Commissioner for National Minorities. The various international agreements it has signed are even incorporated into the Ukrainian law code. Article 4 of the Law on Citizenship reads: 'If an international agreement requires Ukraine to alter some of the paragraphs in this law, they will be changed in accordance with the international agreement.'[46] Signing international agreements on human rights does not guarantee that they will be implemented; however, such agreements do constitute structural constraints on state behaviour, since acting in defiance of them is likely to result in international sanctions. When Ukraine was admitted to the Council of Europe on 9 November 1995, as the second of the CIS countries (after Moldova) to join, its entry indicated the Council of Europe's satisfaction with Ukraine's minority policy.

Ideological factors

Domestic political stability is promoted if a society has some affective foundations – such as patriotism – that hold the community together.[47] The cultivation of such bonds is important in Ukraine today since the non-affective foundation of economic satisfaction is so far very poor. In this respect the most prominent question is: what definition of the Ukrainian nation is dominant in the political discourse? More specifically, is the dominating definition inclusive or exclusive of the Russian minority? If the Russian minority is to share in any affective foundation of Ukrainian independence, the definition will have to be inclusive.

Normally an inclusive definition of the nation is territorial and an exclusive one is ethnic. The definition of the Ukrainian nation dominant in the political discourse since independence has been made both by reference to Ukraine as the state of the ethnic Ukrainians and by reference to territory. Ukrainians are expected by the authorities to ascribe legitimacy to the state both because they are Ukrainians and because they inhabit the territory of Ukraine. Russians are expected to ascribe legitimacy to the state because they inhabit the territory of Ukraine and because they are catered for through minority guarantees. This 'largely territorial with an ethnic element' definition was promoted by the *shestydesyatnyky*[48] and became the official line under Kravchuk.

One of the main historical and ideological sources of this definition of the Ukrainian nation is twentieth-century Ukraine's leading political philosopher, Vyacheslav Lypynsky.[49] According to Alexander Motyl, 'At present, most Ukrainian elites in and out of elective office appear to share at least some of Lypynsky's views.'[50] Lypynsky considered national territory, and not language or other cultural attributes, to be the most essential defining factor of a nation. According to Eugene Pyziur, 'He felt that this would replace nationalism with patriotism, which he equated with what may conditionally be called *Heimatliebe*.'[51] He emphasized the possibility of territory as the basis for a definition of the Ukrainian nation.

> He considered nationalism, operating from the concept of nation based on ethnicity (race, language, culture, religion, or all these elements together), as especially dangerous in the case of Ukraine. In view of the presence on its territory of sizeable minorities, occupying positions of political, cultural, or economic authority, the unleashing of ethnic-based nationalism would oblige these minorities to oppose the idea of statehood for the Ukraine and would compel them to turn to the Russian or Polish metropolis for support.[52]

The official terminology also reflects the teaching of Lypynsky. The new Ukrainian constitution opens by declaring that the Ukrainian parliament adopted this constitution 'in the name of the Ukrainian people – citizens of Ukraine of every nationality'.[53] By choosing such expressions, the official terminology symbolically gives preference to a non-ethnic definition of the state.

Ivan Dzyuba, who in late 1992 was appointed Ukrainian minister of culture, outlined his definition of the Ukrainian nation in the following way: 'Nations are in a state of permanent transformation, and only then are they viable. Perhaps, today, a qualitatively new Ukrainian nation is formed – formed not on the principle of ethnicity, but on the principle of citizenship.'[54] Dzyuba's 'new Ukrainian nation' echoes Lypynsky's territorial concept; it is also noteworthy that Dzyuba specifically refers to Lypynsky as a source of inspiration in this article.[55]

However, this largely territorial definition of the Ukrainian nation did not mean that the *shestydesyatnyky* and the Kravchuk administration were indifferent to the revival of Ukrainian language and culture. State-sponsored measures to promote Ukrainian language, culture and history were implemented, for example in the educational system and in the army. The inclination both to include the Russians in the 'Ukrainian nation' and at the same time to consider them as different from ethnic Ukrainians is well illustrated by the following sentences from the 1991 Rukh programme:

Rukh is hoping that the Russians living in the republic will take part in the present Ukrainian national revival. While respecting the Russian language and culture, and the century-long connections between the Russian and the Ukrainian peoples, Rukh considers that the Russians can only develop as a distinguishable part of the republic's *sotsium* [here meaning community] when a total revival of the Ukrainian nation is also taking place.[56]

This definition of the Ukrainian nation was not challenged by the Kuchma administration. Under Kuchma less emphasis was laid on ethnic Ukrainian national revival, but the understanding of the Ukrainian nation remained basically the same. The minister for nationalities, Volodymyr Yevtukh, affirmed in June 1996 that he conceives of the nation as a political and not an ethnic concept: 'And this means that there has to be an ethnic core around which circle the representatives of other nationalities. The only such core for us is the Ukrainian people. In this situation, the national idea becomes, as the Americans say, mainstream – that is, the main current into which all the smaller currents of the other nationalities are included.'[57]

Russia and the Russian minority in Ukraine

The necessity of defending ethnic Russians in the 'near abroad' if they are threatened is one of the few issues on which there is virtual unanimity among Russian politicians. However, when it comes to ways of doing this, the Russian political establishment can roughly be divided into two groups: those who think that the rights of the Russian minorities can be defended within a system of independent states and those who do not. The Yeltsin administration subscribes to the former position, but is nevertheless prepared to go to considerable lengths to protect ethnic Russians abroad. Foreign minister Andrey Kozyrev stated in April 1995 that Russia has the right to use its military to defend ethnic Russians living abroad.[58] The borderline between these two groups also seems blurred, since even the fairly liberal Moscow mayor, Yury Luzhkov, one of President Yeltsin's closest associates, declared when visiting Sevastopol on 23 December 1994: 'We relate to Sevastopol as to the eleventh district of Moscow, no matter how many customs and border barriers there are. The desire of most of its inhabitants to be and feel Russian must not be suppressed.'[59]

There are at least four reasons why Russia has not played the ESU card, despite these attitudes. First, few Russian politicians seem to fear that the

Russians in Ukraine will suffer discrimination. Russia has put pressure on the Ukrainian authorities to grant the opportunity for dual citizenship, and would like the Russian language to have official status in Ukraine; beyond these suggestions, the fate of Russians in Ukraine has not loomed large in Russian–Ukrainian relations. It is also likely that the relatively rougher treatment experienced by Russian minorities elsewhere, for example in the Baltic republics, has shown Ukraine in a favourable light.

Second, there is a clear recognition among large parts of the Russian political elite that separatist or irredentist efforts in Ukraine could spark a civil war in the country. This would create a massive inflow of refugees to Russia and endanger both Russian domestic political stability and the Russian reform process. Vyacheslav Irgunov, responsible for policy towards Ukraine in the Russian duma committee for CIS matters, said in July 1994: ' I am absolutely convinced that Russia will be careful in her policy towards Ukraine. The important thing for us is that there is civic peace in Ukraine. It is impossible to imagine that there can be stability in Russia, if there is civil war in Ukraine.'[60]

Third, reintegration of Ukraine or parts of Ukraine would most probably deal a hard blow to the Russian treasury.

Fourth, Russia's relations both with the West and with its European neighbours would be seriously worsened if Russia, by encouraging separatist movements, put the territorial integrity of Ukraine at risk. This argument would, of course, become weaker if Russia's relations with the West were to deteriorate for other reasons.

Summary

The absence of ethnic mobilization among the Russians of eastern and southern Ukraine can be attributed only in part to the accommodating minority policy of the Ukrainian state and Moscow's policy of restraint. One can easily find examples of minorities mobilizing against very accommodating nationalizing states and of minorities mobilizing despite being discouraged by the state leadership of their historical homeland. In addition, ethnic mobilization would seem likely given that opinion polls show that a majority of the Russians in ESU feel alienated in, and are dissatisfied with, independent Ukraine. The fact that they have not mobilized for a reunification of the old union or a separation of ESU from the rest of Ukraine can be attributed to features of the minority itself. I have pointed to three such features as essential contributory reasons for the lack of mobilization.

First, both the self-defined ethnic identity and the political loyalty of the Russians of ESU have been in flux since 1991. What the final distribution will be between Ukrainian, Russian and regional self-defined ethnic identities and political loyalties remains to be seen. However, even if both a Russian self-defined ethnic identity and a political loyalty towards Russia should become dominant at the public level – the situation offering the highest potential for ethnic mobilization – the effect would be moderated by the pro-Ukrainian political loyalty prevailing within the ESU political and economic elite.

Second, Russians in Ukraine are not seriously disadvantaged economically or politically. Russians have practically the same career opportunities as Ukrainians, though knowledge of the Ukrainian language will increasingly become required in the highest positions. Economic hardships are suffered fairly equally by Ukrainian regions. However, ESU in general pays more to the federal budget than other regions; and Russians of ESU also compare themselves with the Russians in Russia. Today there is a widespread feeling among Russians of ESU that their living standard is lower than for the Russians across the border. A feeling that the gap is widening, especially if combined with a continued redistribution of wealth in Ukraine to ESU's disadvantage, could be a source of ethnic mobilization in the future.

Third, rational calculation of the anticipated costs and benefits of mobilizing for anti-independence, separatist or extensive autonomist demands leads many Russians of ESU to the conclusion that the costs are too great. Fear of violent conflict, fuelled in part by observation of separatist experiences in other parts of the former Soviet Union, and the risk of a return to old-style Communist politics, also figure in the calculations. Besides, most Russians of ESU still probably feel that it is uncertain to what degree Ukraine will be able to preserve its independence.

B. CRIMEA

Ever since Ukraine became independent Crimea has been considered to be potentially the most dangerous trouble spot in the country. There are two main political conflicts rooted in Crimea. The first is between its Russian majority and the Ukrainian central authorities,[61] and involves cultural, economic, territorial and political demands. The second is between the Crimean Russians and the returned Crimean Tatars. Here the bone of contention is the system of representation of the different ethnic groups in the official political organs of Crimea, the status of the Tatar language and the distribution of land. This conflict is therefore cultural, economic and political but not territorial, since the Tatars do not demand any specific part of Crimea for themselves.

Simferopol versus Kiev

The status of Crimea – as a part of Ukraine or even separate from Ukraine – has been the subject of a constant tug of war between Kiev and the Crimean capital Simferopol.

Crimea's relationship with Ukrainian authorities has gone through four stages since the demise of the Soviet Union in 1991: a period of demands and compromise from 1991 to February 1994; a fast-growing mood of separatism from February 1994 to March 1995; the subjugation of the separatists and their local defeat from March 1995 to July 1995; and a renewed struggle for a comprehensive autonomy deal since summer 1995.

Demands and compromise

Demands for a separate status for Crimea started to appear immediately after the Ukrainian declaration of independence on 24 August 1991. The next day the Republican Movement of Crimea (RMC) was formed, with the task of promoting Crimean secession from Ukraine. It proposed that, following secession, citizens would vote to decide whether Crimea should become an independent state or join Russia. On 4 September 1991 the local legislature, the Crimean Supreme Soviet, declared the state sovereignty of Crimea as a constituent part of Ukraine. The RMC then started to campaign for a referendum on the question of independence. It persuaded the Crimean parliament to adopt a law providing for a referendum in November 1991, and within months it had gathered close to 250,000 signatures in favour of holding such a referendum.

The Ukrainian parliament had recognized the autonomous status of Crimea on paper as early as February 1991, after a Crimean referendum in January 1991 had shown that 93 per cent of the Crimean population was in favour of autonomy. It was still unclear, however, what powers the Ukrainian central government would bestow to Crimea. Kiev's response to the demand for a referendum was to start negotiations with the political leadership in Crimea. These negotiations led to the draft of a law 'On the Delineation of Power between Ukraine and the Republic of Crimea'. After this draft had been presented to both the Crimean and the Kiev parliaments, and several amendments had been made to reach compromises on the remaining points at issue, the Ukrainian parliament on 30 June passed the law, now entitled 'On the Delineation of Power between the Organs of State Rule of Ukraine and Crimea'. This law provided the main guidelines for the relationship until the separatist electoral landslide in February 1994.

Since 1991 politics in Crimea has been dominated by the Russophone parties, the Communists and the business parties. The Russophone parties comprise a group of small parties that advocate some form of union with Russia and the dominant Crimean Republican Party, which wants Crimea to be an independent state. Before the 1994 parliamentary elections these parties formed the Rossiya (Russia) parliamentary block. In 1994 Rossiya split into three factions when some deputies dissatisfied with its low profile on economic reform broke away and formed the Reformy (Reforms) faction. Then, after Crimean President Yuriy Meshkov's unsuccessful attempt to dissolve the Crimean parliament in September 1994, those members of Rossiya still loyal to Meshkov formed their own faction, Rossiya-Yedinstvo (Russia-Unity).

The Communist Party of Crimea was established in June 1992. Initially opposed to reform and in favour of restoration of the Soviet Union, it eventually dropped its pro-USSR position but remained anti-reform. It still advocates close cooperation among the former Soviet republics, but party leader Leonid Grach said in May 1995: 'We cannot go back to the old Soviet Union. People would not put up with it.'[62]

Business interests are represented by the Union for the Support of the Republic of Crimea (USRC) and the Party for Economic Renaissance of Crimea (PERC). USRC represents the managers of Crimean heavy industry, largely dependent on the flow of subsidies from Kiev and therefore sceptical about Crimean independence. PERC is a market-reform-orientated party advocating economic but not political independence for Crimea. It represents the branches of Crimean trade and industry with the most promising economic prospects, such as the sanatoria along the southern coastline. The party held its first congress in 1993 and by early 1994 had already become 'the most powerful party in Crimea, and the one with the strongest links with the local economic and political establishment'.[63] Since then its influence has increased, and in October 1995 PERC entered an alliance with the Ukrainian Liberal Party. This party includes, as mentioned before, a number of the most prominent pro-independence, pro-economic reform politicians in Ukraine, and has good contacts with the Kuchma administration. The alliance therefore further strengthened PERC's influence in Kiev. In March 1996 PERC registered as an all-Ukrainian party and removed 'Crimea' from the party's name, so that the abbreviation is now PER.

Growing separatism

Candidates of the Rossiya political coalition won both the presidential elections in January 1994 and the parliamentary elections in March with 51 seats out of a total of 94, creating a seemingly united drive for greater independence. President Meshkov turned the clocks in Crimea to Moscow time, stated that Crimeans should serve their military service only in Crimea, demanded the removal of all Ukrainian troops and military installations from Crimea and reactivated the strongly pro-independence 1992 Crimean constitution. One of the Crimean leadership's main threats during the whole period was to hold a referendum on the separation issue. In September the parliament discussed the following wording for the referendum: 'Are you in favour of the Independent Republic of Crimea, in a union with other states?'[64]

Initially, Kiev met these and other actions with no more than verbal condemnation. A war of decrees developed that totally overshadowed the occasional attempts at negotiations. The atmosphere in Crimea was one of exhilaration; the Crimean parliamentary Speaker, Sergey Tsekov, confidently stated: 'We are not ignoring Kiev, and we are not threatening Ukraine's territorial integrity, we are only realizing the programme of Crimean and Russian reunion.'[65]

Subjugation and local defeat

The champions of Crimean independence suffered three serious setbacks during spring and early summer 1995: Kiev issued several decrees severely limiting Crimean autonomy; the Crimean leadership – already entrenched in internal feuds – after initial protests backed down and accepted most of Kiev's demands; and on 5 July, Sergey Tsekov, front figure of the separatist Rossiya parliamentary faction and leader of the Crimean Republican Party as well as Speaker, lost a vote of confidence in the Crimean parliament. To replace him as Speaker the parliament elected Evgeniy Suprunyuk, who was conciliatory towards Kiev.

Kiev dealt the first major blow to Crimean autonomy on 17 March 1995 when the Ukrainian parliament, with a large majority, annulled the 1992 Crimean constitution and, among other things, rendered the Crimean presidency void. Thirteen days later President Kuchma issued a decree placing the Crimean government directly under the Ukrainian government, thus denying the Crimean parliament any control over its own executive. These actions were the first serious deviations from the fairly cautious line Kiev had taken on Crimean separatism since Ukrainian independence in 1991. What prompted the change of policy? There are three key factors: the improbability of Russian involvement; the presence of reliable allies in Crimea; and the internal turmoil and divisions within the separatist Crimean leadership.

First, the Yeltsin leadership has made few attempts to interfere in Ukrainian–Crimean relations, despite the fact that 70 per cent of the Crimean population is Russian and Crimea is the base of the Black Sea Fleet. President Yeltsin and other leading figures in the Russian administration have repeatedly stated that Crimea is internal Ukrainian business. There are, however, strong pro-Crimean sentiments within the Russian political elite and among the Russian population,[66] and it is not possible for any Russian administration to turn its back on developments in Crimea. Yeltsin's international aide, Dmitriy Ryurikov, reacted to the Ukrainian parliament's annulling of the 1992 Crimean constitution by telling *Izvestiya* on 21 March 1995: 'Events in Crimea are Ukraine's internal affair. However, for well-known reasons the Russian leadership would like the adoption of these decisions to have no result in conflicts *that Russia would have to get involved in settling*' (emphasis added).[67]

Because Ukraine could not be sure of Russian non-involvement, it was important for President Kuchma to initiate the new policy at a point when the likelihood of this occurring was at its lowest. The war in Chechenia provided such an opportunity. It would not be easy for Yeltsin to condemn Kiev for solving its problems with a separatist province by juridical means while simultaneously bombing out the Chechen separatism in Russia's own backyard. In addition, a display of military strength to deter Kiev would be more difficult now than before the Chechen war. Yevhen Zherebetsky, a member of the Ukrainian parliamentary commission on Foreign and CIS affairs, explicitly asserted such reasoning as a major factor behind Kiev's firmer line towards Crimea.[68]

Second, by March 1995 Kiev could rely on two allies in Crimea: a considerable part of the former administrative and economic nomenklatura, and the Crimean law-enforcement structures, which Kiev had long been cultivating. Reaching an accommodation with the Crimean nomenklatura was one of Kiev's main strategies in stabilizing the conflict with Crimea. The former Crimean Speaker of parliament, Nikolay Bagrov, was pivotal in this work. Before the January 1994 elections this strategy seemed to be succeeding, and, since most observers expected Bagrov to win the Crimean presidential election, to be likely to continue to succeed.

However, the landslide victory in the Crimean presidential election for Yuriy Meshkov, who took 73 per cent of the vote against Bagrov's 23 per cent, changed the picture entirely.[69] The Crimean political and economic nomenklatura was essentially deprived of political power on the peninsula when Meshkov's victory in the presidential election in January was followed by victory for his parliamentary bloc – Rossiya – in the parliamentary elections in March. Nevertheless, Kiev continued to nurture its relationship with the Crimean nomenklatura throughout 1994. The fruitfulness of this policy was demonstrated by the fact that Kiev's decisive steps in March were preceded by an appeal from the mayors of most Crimean towns and the directors of 68 of the largest companies of Crimea, calling on Kuchma to 'stop the political boozing session on the peninsula'.[70]

Control over the law enforcement structures is a prerequisite for anybody wanting to have a say in Crimean politics, and by March 1995 most of these structures were firmly in Kiev's hands. From Kiev's point of view, among Meshkov's most provocative steps as president were his assumption of authority over the Crimean militia and his appointment of Valeriy Kuznetsov – a general sacked from the Ukrainian armed forces for lack of patriotism – as Crimean minister of the interior. The former step was, however, quickly and successfully reversed by the Kiev-appointed militia general Valery Chernyshov, and since autumn 1994 a reorganization and resubordination under Kiev of all interior ministry structures in Crimea has taken place. Delegations from the Ukrainian ministry of the interior and from the Ukrainian security service have been present on the peninsula more or less constantly, their activities directed by the former chief of the Ukrainian security service and Ukrainian prime minister, Yevhen Marchuk.

Third, Kiev was encouraged to take a harder line by the split in the separatist leadership, which made it less capable of opposing Kiev; the turmoil in the leadership had led to Crimean politics being more or less hamstrung since autumn 1994. By autumn 1994 Meshkov and his confederates of the Rossiya parliamentary block had so fallen out with one another that Meshkov tried forcefully, but unsuccessfully, to dissolve the Rossiya-dominated Crimean parliament. Parliament and president became preoccupied with sorting out their relationship, and simultaneously the work of the legislature became more and more a farce – as illustrated by the fact that one of the issues occupying much of the parliamentarians' time from autumn 1994 onwards was whether or not a tiny village outside the city of Belogorsk should be joined with Belogorsk, while the debate on the 1995 Crimean budget was found so uninteresting by the Crimean deputies that only a quarter of them turned up for the voting, rendering the parliament unable to adopt a budget.

Most observers agree that what undermined the cohesion of the Rossiya block was the question of property; or rather the *division* of property.[71] Despite the all-Ukrainian moratorium on privatization from September 1994, politicians in Crimea were trying to exploit their positions to privatize enterprises in their own favour. The former prime minister Saburov made attempts to privatize several major and undoubtedly lucrative sanatoria along the southern coastline. Similarly, President Meshkov, after subordinating the Crimean State Property Fund to himself, insisted on selling several of the highly profitable Crimean ports into private hands. The port in Feodosia alone brings in close to $1 million a month.[72] Though relations between politicians and business (some would say mafia) circles in Crimea are shrouded in secrecy, few observers doubt their existence and decisive influence. It is arguable whether the conflict between the Crimean president and the parliament can be explained exclusively by their divergent economic interests, but there are few other plausible explanations for the clash between a president and a parliament with nearly identical positions on most other major issues. One observer, Valeriy Zaytsev, has gone so far as to talk about 'the personal and "bonapartistic" ambitions of the Crimean politicians, who represent the economic interests of mafia clans'.[73]

Crimean leaders protested against the decisions handed down from Kiev in late March 1995. Parliamentary Speaker Tsekov raged: 'Crimea is turned not just into an ordinary province of Ukraine, but into a colony. This decision proves that Ukraine is an authoritarian state with a police regime.'[74] President Meshkov locked himself up in his office and continued this protest in solitude until 11 June, when he was hospitalized with diphtheria. The Crimean parliament decided to hold a referendum on the issue of a Slavic union with Russia and Belarus.

However, by early June the Crimean legislators seemed to be retreating on most fronts. The proposed referendum, scheduled for 25 June, was called off on 15 June. The parliament, under strong pressure from Speaker Tsekov, also passed in a first reading the text for the new Crimean constitution, from which most of the separatist wording of the 1992 Crimean constitution was absent.[75]

At least three factors are central to explaining this retreat by the Crimean leadership. The first and most urgent is that the Crimean legislators were willing to pay a high price – such as erasing the separatist claims of the 1992 constitution – to get the Crimean government back under their control. The idea of privatization in Crimea being carried out by a government controlled from Kiev was unbearable to most deputies in the Crimean parliament. The leader of the Rossiya-Yedinstvo faction, Yuriy Zyryanov, bluntly stated that it was necessary to cancel the planned referendum because 'in Crimea a government not controlled by us is operating, and privatization is about to start.'[76] The Crimean parliament got its government back on 8 June, when President Kuchma overturned his previous decision to place the Crimean government directly under the all-Ukrainian government. This was done after assurances from the Crimean authorities that the 25 June referendum would be cancelled.

Second, despite numerous missions and appeals to Russia by Crimean parliamentarians, and speeches by Crimean leaders in the Russian duma, Russia did not give Crimea economic and political backing for the planned referendum, thereby leaving the parliamentarians with no funds to conduct it. In fact, the economy was in such a pitiful state that, according to Ukrainian minister of finance Mykola Syvulskiy, Crimea had become one of the most subsidized regions in Ukraine.[77] It was therefore in a weak bargaining position *vis-à-vis* Kiev, given both its financial dependence on Ukraine and the lack of financial or political backing from Russia.

Third, the Crimean authorities did not get the support they had hoped for at the OSCE conference on Crimean problems – initiated largely by Simferopol – in Locarno on 11–14 June 1995. Though the OSCE warned Kiev against provocative steps, such as disbanding the Crimean parliament, it showed little sympathy for the claim of the Crimean people to determine the status of the peninsula. The outcome of the Locarno conference was therefore a great disappointment for the Crimean leaders. The leader of the Rossiya-Yedinstvo faction, Zyryanov, could see only one reason for the OSCE's uncomprehending attitude: 'the desire of certain groupings of the West to hinder Ukrainian–Russian rapprochement'.[78]

Once Meshkov and Rossiya came to power in early 1994, they kept few of their pre-election promises. No pensions were paid in roubles, living conditions continued to deteriorate and crime was worse than ever. Crimean voters probably perceived their government's submission to demands from Kiev as the final proof that the pro-Russian parties in the Rossiya coalition were unable to fulfil their promises. This perception can be seen clearly in the catastrophic showing of Tsekov's Republican Party in the Crimean municipal elections of 25 June, when it won only five seats in the municipal councils, compared to the Communists' 290. Tsekov lost the vote of confidence on 5 July because several deputies from Rossiya shifted their allegiance and joined the parliamentary opposition. Though their official explanation for this defection was that Tsekov had concentrated too much power in his own hands and become too compliant towards Kiev, the definite show of distrust for the pro-Russian forces in the municipal elections was probably of equal importance.

When the Crimean parliament got its government back, it was with the serious limitation that future candidates for the prime minister's post had to be approved by the Ukrainian president. At the same time Kuchma further strengthened Kiev's control by placing Crimean local administrative structures under the central Ukrainian government, and by merging the Crimean privatization bureau with the local branch of the Ukrainian privatization bureau.

The factional structure of the Crimean parliament also underwent serious changes as a result of the surrender to Kiev. The former majority Rossiya faction was left with only ten deputies, whereas the new faction supporting Suprunyuk, Creation, emerged as the strongest with 23 deputies. Creation has brought together former enemies. It is led by Vladimir Shevev from PERC, and can count both the former Rossiya leader, Sergey Nikulin, and Vadim Mordashov from the Republican Movement of Crimea in its ranks.

Renewed tug of war

In autumn 1995 the new Crimean command, led by Suprunyuk and strongly supported by PER, embarked upon a three-pronged strategy: to assure Kiev that the separatist threat was over; to assure the majority Russian population of Crimea that Crimea would get a substantial autonomy deal through the adoption of a Crimean constitution; and to ensure that they gained control over economic policy and privatization. Only the first of these aims was easily secured.

After the reshuffle of the Crimean parliament in June 1995, the parliament started to draw up a new Crimean constitution. This document was adopted by the Crimean parliament on 1 November 1995, and sent to the Ukrainian parliament for approval. The Ukrainian parliament, however, was in no hurry to bestow this. In particular, it did not want to adopt the Crimean constitution before the Ukrainian one, since doing this would considerably limit the scope for formulating the article on Crimea in the latter. Several of its committees, however, did examine the Crimean proposal. By the time the Ukrainian parliament adopted this proposal in the first reading on 20 March 1996, these committees had accumulated a list of 252 proposed changes. A number of formulations were especially unacceptable to Kiev, and had to be changed before the Ukrainian parliament would be willing to adopt the Crimean constitution in the second reading: 'citizen of Crimea' to 'citizen of Ukraine living in Crimea'; 'the Crimean people' to 'the population of Crimea'; 'the Republic of Crimea' to 'the Autonomous Republic of Crimea'; Ukrainian and Tatar had to be named as official languages alongside Russian; and Crimea was to have no flag, coats of arms or anthem.[79]

The new Crimean government was irritated both by what they saw as dawdling on the constitutional issue, and by the extent of the changes demanded. A combination of irritation with Kiev and a need to accommodate the growing anti-Kiev popular mood at home made the new rulers increasingly more outspoken against Kiev in the course of the autumn of 1995. In March 1996 the Speaker of parliament, Suprunyuk, accused Kiev of betrayal and said that he had made a mistake when he initially believed everything said in Kiev.[80] Later the same month, while in Kiev, he threatened to remove the moratorium on the referendum on the status of the peninsula. The new tone from Crimea provoked the official representative of the president in the Ukrainian parliament, Victor Musiyaka, to state angrily that to accept the Autonomous Republic of Crimea had been a political mistake all along.[81]

The new Crimean government's aim of securing control over economic policy and privatization was complicated by the lack of a Crimean constitution. The Crimean government has already formulated a major programme for large-scale privatization, but the constitution has to be in place before it can be implemented. A further source of irritation for the Crimean leadership was its suspicion that Kiev was holding back on the constitutional issue on purpose, so that it could conduct privatization in Crimea itself. In February 1996 two Crimean sanatoria were deducted from the Crimean list of enterprises for privatization, and put under Kiev's control.[82] Suprunyuk complained that Kiev was not keeping its promises not to redistribute Crimean property.[83]

At the time of writing the Crimean constitution had still not been adopted by the Ukrainian parliament, but Crimea did secure its status as an Autonomous Republic in the Ukrainian constitution adopted by parliament in June 1996.[84]

The return of the Tatars

When the Golden Horde disintegrated in the middle of the fifteenth century, the Tatars in Crimea formed their own khanate in 1443. From 1478 this khanate survived as a semi-independent state under Ottoman suzerainty until Russia under Catherine II conquered it in 1783. Except for a brief interlude from November 1917 to January 1918 the Tatars were never again masters of the peninsula, and in May 1944 most Crimean Tatars (about 188,000) were deported to Central Asia on allegations of cooperation with the Nazi forces. Whenever politically possible during the postwar period the Tatars campaigned for their right to return, which was granted in July 1988.

Since then a steady stream of Tatars has returned to Crimea. In the last Soviet census in 1989, there were 38,365 Tatars living in Crimea, making up 1.5 per cent of the population.[85] The peak of repatriation was in 1992 and 1993, when about 80,000 a year returned. Since then the influx has slowed down considerably, and in June 1995 an estimated 240,000 Crimean Tatars were living in Crimea.[86]

The poor integration of the Crimean Tatars into Crimean political and economic life constitutes one of the most serious dangers to political stability for the peninsula.

Tatar organizations

From the very beginning of their return the Tatars have organized themselves in order to improve their conditions. There are now four main political parties representing them. The most influential is the Organization of the Crimean Tatar National Movement (OCNM),[87] which is the leading force in the unofficial Tatar parliament, the Medzhlis. The 33-member Medzhlis was elected at the first all-union congress (Kurultay) of Crimean Tatars in Simferopol on 29 June 1992 and half of its representatives are members of OCNM.[88] The OCNM at its congress in January 1993 stated as the organization's main goal 'to return and settle the Crimean-Tatar people in its homeland, and to re-establish its national statehood'.[89] Despite the widespread use of such phrases, OCNM is a relatively moderate political party. Its undisputed leader, Refat Chubarov, who is a widely respected politician both in Crimea and in Kiev, is a major architect of this moderate policy. After Supryunuk was elected the new speaker of the Crimean parliament, Chubarov was elected as one of three deputy speakers. Chubarov also played a crucial role in calming the Tatar population after the clashes between Tatars and Ukrainian special forces in June 1995.

The National Movement of Crimean Tatars (NMCT), established as early as 1967, has traditionally been less radical in its demands and more cooperative towards the Russian majority, and thus distrusted by the other Tatar political parties. The NMCT today plays only a minor role in Crimean politics.

A radical Tatar organization called Milli Firka (National Party) was established in July 1993 by Ilmy Umerov, the Medzhlis' representative in the town of Bakhchisarai.[90] Its aim is 'the establishment of an independent, ethnic Crimean Tatar state in which the indigenous people will receive priority'.[91] It argues for the Crimean Tatar language to be the only state language and announces its readiness to use 'all means necessary' to achieve its goals.[92]

A new nationalist Tatar party under the name of Adalet (Justice) was formed on 19 August 1995 under the leadership of Server Kerimov. Adalet seeks Crimean autonomy within Ukraine and the introduction of the Islamic Shari'a law on the peninsula. At the end of 1995 there were reports of Adalet organizing joint combat training for its adherents together with the paramilitary wing of the small extreme nationalistic Ukrainian party, State Independence for Ukraine.[93]

Both Milli Firka and Adalet attract comparatively little support among the Tatars and the OCNM today enjoys a very prominent position as spokesman for the Crimean Tatars.

Sources of Tatar frustration

Tatars' frustrations stems from three main sources: socio-economic grievances, political grievances and the feeling of historical injustice.

(1) Socio-economic grievances The social situation for the returned Tatars is far from simple. Infant mortality is three times higher than the Ukrainian average, and 40 per cent of adults are unemployed.[94] The majority of the returned Tatars are farmers, and the land question is therefore a key issue. According to one estimate, up to 80 per cent of the Tatar population live from trade at the local markets.[95] Farm produce is their main commodity. In 1993 the Crimean authorities tried unsuccessfully to pass a land privatization law, justifying the Tatars' long-held fear that their land needs would be ignored. The Crimean authorities have made some concessions to the Tatars on this issue. At the end of March 1993, a law 'On the provision of land for the resettlement of deported people' was adopted. This law instructed the local councils in six towns in eastern

Crimea to appropriate a total of 35,000 hectares of land for the settlement of Tatars.[96] However, this was far from enough to satisfy the Tatars. The land issue was the direct cause of the first violent conflict between them and the Crimean authorities when, in October 1992, some Tatars who in desperation had put up their tents in the middle of a peach-garden near the town of Alushta clashed with police.[97]

However, the conflict between the Tatars and Crimean mafia groupings has proved the most explosive. During spring 1995 the level of tension between Tatars selling their produce at local markets and Crimean mafia groups regularly demanding protection money increased significantly. In April one Tatar was brutally murdered. At the end of June two more Tatars were beaten to death by the mafia because they refused to pay protection money. When the news spread, Tatars from all over Crimea gathered to avenge the murders. In the town of Sudak, they were blocked by a Ukrainian special forces unit or *Berkuta*. The special forces fired at the crowd: two Tatars were killed and many more wounded. Only after numerous appeals by Tatar leaders did the raging crowd disperse. This incident was the most serious case of civil disturbance in Ukraine since independence. There is naturally a danger of such incidents radicalizing the Tatars, possibly increasing support for organizations such as Milli Firka and Adalet. Unless the mafia is brought under control, this might further erode the Tatars' trust in Crimean local authorities and Kiev, as the Tatars will blame them for not taking effective action.

The June 1995 clashes discredited both the Ukrainian central authorities and Crimean local authorities. The Berkuta platoon was under Kievan control, while the local authorities must bear a large part of the responsibility for not cracking down earlier on the local mafia. In any case, it is likely that this episode strengthened Kiev's determination to secure political control in Crimea. Further clashes could seriously harm Ukraine's image as one of the most stable successor states of the Soviet Union.

(2) Political grievances In pursuit of a voice in Crimean politics, in 1991 the Tatars proposed a bicameral system, consisting of a 100-strong lower chamber elected from territorial constituencies and a 50-strong upper chamber, the Medzhlis. Thus the Tatars would be able to veto decisions in the Crimean parliament that were not to their liking. The Crimean leadership, as expected, rejected the proposal. After long negotiations and protests and demonstrations by Tatars – including blocking of railway lines – the Crimean Supreme Soviet agreed on 14 October 1993 to a

special Tatar quota of 14 out of 96 seats in the parliament. Though this was a partial victory for the Tatars, other unmet political demands have continued to fuel their dissatisfaction. First, Kiev has so far not recognized the Medzhlis as the official representative assembly of the Tatars. Second, Kiev's annulment of the Crimean constitution on 17 March 1995, though in general supported by the Tatars, also eliminated the Tatar quotas in parliament. Kiev then did little to make sure that these quotas were reinstated. In November 1995 ten Tatar parliamentary deputies went on hunger strike to campaign for the restoration of fixed quotas for the Tatars in the Crimean parliament.

Another complaint is that about 60,000 of the returned Tatars have not been accorded Ukrainian citizenship because they lack documentation to prove that they have renounced their former citizenship. They are therefore unable to vote and possibly also to take part in the planned privatization of state assets.

Though the Tatars are still dissatisfied with the level of political influence they have achieved, they have moderated their demands in this area. When the Crimean parliament discussed the new constitution in June 1995, the Tatar deputy Nadyr Bekirov, on behalf of the Kurultay, once more suggested a bicameral system; but rather than one territorially elected chamber and one Tatar chamber, he proposed one territorially and one nationally elected chamber. A nationally elected chamber would mean that the Tatars would elect deputies from among the Tatar community, the Ukrainians from the Ukrainian community, and so on. Whether the quotas in the nationally elected chamber would be equal for all nationalities, or proportional to each nationality's percentage of the population was, however, unclear. The proposal received little support beyond the Tatar community.

(3) Feeling of historical injustice There is a strong feeling in the Tatar community, maintained throughout the years in exile, that Crimea historically is their land. Even the moderate Medzhlis leader Cemiloglu has stated: 'The whole of Crimea is our land.'[98] Although the Tatar leadership has been considerably more moderate in practical politics than this claim suggests, the idea is probably still strong in the community. As long as Tatars demand the resurrection of the Tatar state of Crimea, their discontent and the potential for conflict with the Slavic population will fester.

In the political realm, because of the still fairly moderate position of the Tatars and the change of leadership in Crimea, there is a possibility for compromise and mutually satisfactory solutions. The Tatars' feeling of historical injustice may diminish given time, the resolution of political demands, and a degree of tact on the part of Russians and Ukrainians towards the Tatars' history.

However, the socio-economic problems are political dynamite. Unemployment, lack of housing, lack of land, maltreatment by the mafia and the widespread opinion that the law enforcement structures are on the mafia's side has created a feeling among Tatars that they are being forced into a corner. In the longer run the Tatar–mafia conflict could also escalate into an ethnic conflict between the Tatars and the Russians, if the former came to see mafia violence as just an expression of a general hatred of them on the part of the Russian population.

Summary

The relationship between the local Crimean authorities and the Ukrainian central authorities has changed dramatically during the period 1991–6. After Crimean separatism became a threat to Ukrainian territorial integrity in 1994, Kiev changed its policy from verbal condemnation to determined action. The Crimean leadership gave in to Kiev's demands and was then overturned at home. Of the three circumstances that were instrumental in this turn of events – Russian non-interference, the Crimean politicians' preoccupation with securing control over the division of Crimean property, and Crimea's financial dependence on Ukraine – all are still influential, but none is permanent, and changes in one or more of these circumstances could easily bring a new wave of Crimean separatism. Russia could change its approach; the separatists could sort out their internal feuds and present new leaders; the pro-Russian parties' defeat in the June 1994 municipal elections might reflect a mistrust more of the leaders of these parties than of their ideas; and once the Crimean economy starts working, Crimea's financial dependence on Ukraine could lessen. There are signs that the Crimean Communists – increasingly self-confident after their very good showing in the 1994 municipal elections – are considering a return to their pro-Russian course.

For the champions of Crimean independence therefore, the events of March 1995 probably represent more a temporary defeat than a resignation to the fate of being forever part of independent Ukraine. As the deputy Speaker of the Crimean parliament, Victor Mezhak, stated after parliament changed the wording of the constitution: 'We are for the time being forced to hide our pro-Russian principles and wait for more favourable conditions.'[99]

The most immediate danger to political stability on the peninsula is posed by the Tatars. Their repatriation, incorporation into Crimean economic and political life, and cooperation with the majority Slavic population are crucial issues that the Ukrainian central authorities and Crimean local authorities must solve.

Despite the successful suppression of Crimean separatism, Crimean ethnic passion is one of the most serious challenges to Ukrainian political stability.

Chapter 4

Ukraine and Russia

'The awakening of Ukraine, and especially the separatist character of Ukrainianness, surprised the Russian intelligentsia, and we were never able to understand it. This was first of all, because we loved Ukraine, we loved her land, her people, her songs, and we thought that all this was also part of our national heritage. Also, the separatism was incomprehensible to us because we had never really been interested in the three to four centuries of history that had formed the Ukrainian people and their culture different from the Great Russians.' – GEORGIY FEDOTOV (1886–1951)[1]

Although this passage was written in 1947 by the Russian philosopher and social scientist Georgiy Fedotov, it is a good description of how many Russians felt in 1991 when Ukraine became independent. As Fedotov said: 'The Ukrainian national problem is for Russia more important than any other national question. This is not only a question of Russia's structure or borders, we are here talking about her soul.'[2]

The Kievan Rus state formation (c. 900–1240) is the common heritage for both Russians and Ukrainians. Russians frequently call Kiev the mother of all Russian cities. The Kiev state was crushed by the Mongols in 1240, but from about 1340 the Mongols had to give up their possessions in Ukraine to the expanding Grand Princes of Lithuania. At about the same time the Poles moved into the western Ukrainian provinces of Galicia and Volhynia. This is where Russian and Ukrainian history separate. Russia remained under Mongol rule for another 150 years, whereas Ukraine gradually became part of the Polish-Lithuanian medieval state.

In the middle of the sixteenth century the introduction of serfdom led to a significant increase in the number of so-called Cossacks in the

61

Ukrainian parts of the Polish state. A Cossack was a peasant who preferred the dangerous but free life in the eastern provinces to that of serfhood in the west: a combination of farmer and soldier. The existence of the Cossacks was accepted by the Polish authorities, because they formed a buffer against Tatar raids into the western parts of Ukraine.

Gradually the Cossacks began to organize politically, and in the second half of the sixteenth century the Zaporozhian Sich, a Cossack stronghold on the lower Dniepr, emerged as the centre of the Ukrainian Cossacks. The Zaporozhian Sich soon started to act as a sovereign power, and established foreign policy relations with, among others, the Habsburgs and the Pope in opposition to the Ottomans. In the long run the Cossacks' independent policy could not be tolerated by Poland, and attempts were made to subdue them by force. This led to the famous rebellion of 1648 under the leadership of Bohdan Khmelnytsky, who thereby gained control over most of present-day Ukraine, except the westernmost provinces. The victory was fragile, however, and Khmelnytsky needed a partner to secure his victory. The choice fell upon the Muscovite tsar, and in 1654 the Treaty of Pereiaslav was signed. From this time on, Ukrainian autonomy gradually diminished, and by the time Russian troops destroyed the Zaporozhian Sich in 1775 it had been reduced almost to nothing. Today Ukrainians and Russians argue whether the treaty should be interpreted as only a temporary military agreement, or as the natural reunification of the Ukrainian and Russian peoples.

For both historical and cultural reasons, therefore, Ukrainian independence was harder for many Russians to accept than the independence of most other former Soviet republics.

The purpose of this chapter is to evaluate the current and future potential for conflict between Ukraine and Russia. The chapter is divided into three parts. The first presents the state of Ukrainian–Russian relations since Ukrainian independence. The second evaluates systemic factors and national attributes that are, or are likely to be, influential in shaping the future relationship. Systemic factors include the influence of third countries and the interplay between economic relations and politics. National attributes include foreign policy capabilities and domestic limitations on foreign policy decisions. The third section offers four scenarios of how the relationship might develop under different combinations of what I term moderate and nationalist governments in Ukraine and Russia respectively.

A. PROBLEMS IN UKRAINIAN–RUSSIAN RELATIONS

Four areas have been particularly problematic in the Ukrainian–Russian relationship since Ukraine became independent: Russian acceptance of Ukrainian independence; Ukrainian foreign policy; the division of former Soviet military assets; and Ukrainian territorial integrity.

Russian acceptance of Ukrainian independence

Russian politicians, both in and out of office, who have either rejected or at least shown – in Ukrainian eyes – insufficient respect for Ukrainian independence, have been a constant worry for both the Kravchuk and the Kuchma administrations.

Ukrainian leaders fear that a future Russian government might try to bring Ukraine to its knees. According to a confidential memorandum to President Kuchma from Foreign Minister Udovenko, leaked to the press in October 1995,

> Russia has no intention to build its relations with the CIS countries in line with international law, nor to respect the principles of territorial integrity, sovereignty, and non-interference in domestic affairs ... The integration, proclaimed as useful and necessary in Yeltsin's decree ... in fact means undermining the CIS countries' sovereignty, subordinating their activity to Russia's interests and restoring the centralized superpower.[3]

Ukrainian foreign policy

Two issues in particular have made Ukrainian foreign policy a problem for Russia: Ukraine's resistance to integration in the CIS, and its attempts to lean towards the West in foreign policy. For Russia it is vital that Ukraine does not engage in or promote processes that make Russia more politically remote from western and central Europe, and that it remains within a Russian-dominated community of states. In addition, Russia has increasingly come to worry about Ukraine becoming an impediment to Russian influence in the Black Sea region.

The form of the CIS treaty signed in December 1991 was largely a result of a compromise necessary to obtain Kravchuk's signature. Russia and Belarus could not imagine CIS cooperation without Ukraine, and Kravchuk was therefore in a position to bargain. Under Kuchma, Ukraine has moved from considering the CIS as a 'civilized means of divorce' to seeing it as an acceptable tool for increased economic cooperation. Russian leaders, on the other hand, despite numerous official statements reasserting the centrality of the CIS cooperation (for example, Yeltsin's September 1995 decree on the 'Establishment of the Strategic Course of the Russian Federation with Member States of the CIS'), remain ambivalent towards the CIS.[4] There is little disagreement on the need for integration of the former Soviet republics, but considerable ambiguity about what role the CIS should play in this. Should it be the vehicle of integration, or only one vehicle among several? So far Russia has reached the most important 'integrative' agreements through bilateral negotiations. This has been considered the most efficient way, since it thus avoids the risk of facing collective opposition in the CIS.[5] Its own ambivalence has not, however, reduced Russia's anger over Ukraine's lack of enthusiasm for the CIS, since this lack of enthusiasm is interpreted – correctly – by Moscow as resistance to the idea of integration in general.

Ukraine did not accede to the CIS Interparliamentary Assembly in March 1992, or to the CIS Collective Security Act (the Tashkent Treaty) in May 1992, or to the CIS Charter in February 1993. Finally, distrust of the CIS was formalized as the official Ukrainian strategy in the document 'Fundamental Guidelines in Ukrainian Foreign Policy' adopted by the parliament on 2 July 1993. This document includes the statement: 'Ukraine will avoid participation in the institutionalization of forms of multilateral cooperation within the framework of the CIS which might transform the CIS into a supranational structure of a federal or confederate character.'[6]

The Kuchma administration adopted a more positive stance towards the CIS than the Kravchuk administration had done, but remained cautious towards most integration initiatives. It seems to be guided by three principles. First, Ukraine should take a much more active role in the discussions in the CIS, in order to help shape the organization. Second, Ukraine should stay out of, and work against, any supra-state or executive organs in the CIS. (In September 1994 it chose to be only an associate member of the Inter-State Economic Committee, the first CIS organ with executive powers.) Third, Ukraine should stay away from efforts to achieve coordination in the foreign policy and security fields.[7]

At present Ukraine finds it valuable to be a part of the CIS, both because of the need for economic cooperation and because the CIS provides an arena for dialogue. Whether Ukraine will continue to value it naturally depends upon how the cooperation develops. If it gradually develops into the main vehicle for reintegration of the former Soviet republics under

Russia's control, the chances are that Ukraine will leave and thus create even more tension in relations with Moscow. Even if the political elite in Moscow should come to an agreement on making the CIS the main vehicle for integration, however, this is not certain to come about. First, Russia would have to pay most of the costs of integration. A concrete example is the programme for training CIS officers in Russian military colleges. In February 1996 the Russian ministry of defence announced that these programmes would be cancelled, since the participating CIS countries did not pay for their officers, and the Russian ministry of defence was unable to do so.[8] Second, Ukraine is not alone in its scepticism towards ever greater integration in the CIS. In resisting political and military integration it is joined by Moldova, Azerbaijan and Uzbekistan. This has led to an acceptance within the CIS of different levels of integration. Russia also in practice accepted this – at least temporarily – when it signed an agreement on close integration within the framework of the CIS for only Russia, Belarus, Kazakstan and Kyrgyzstan. If this principle takes hold, it will make it easier for Ukraine to remain a CIS member. It should also be noted that Ukraine's more cooperative spirit in the CIS is being appreciated by Russia. Prime Minister Chernomyrdin said after the March 1996 CIS summit: 'I never saw the Ukrainian delegation working so productively and constructively in helping to find solutions to difficult questions.'[9]

The 'running to the West' started as early as January 1992, when Kravchuk mentioned Poland, Hungary and Canada, but not Russia, as the most likely friends of independent Ukraine.[10] The process of looking westwards started with trade agreements, first with Poland and later with Czechoslovakia and Hungary, and gradually extended to other issues. Agreements on military cooperation were signed with Hungary in March 1992 and with Poland in February 1993. The last – and for Russia most provocative – move was made by Ukraine at the Conference on Security and Cooperation in Europe (CSCE) meeting in Prague in April 1993. Here Ukraine presented a proposal for the creation of a collective security system including central European countries, the Baltic states and Ukraine, but not Russia and Belarus.

Nevertheless, the westward orientation under Kravchuk was more about declamations than about real achievements. Kuchma, once in power, achieved much more in relations with the West. Though he argued in his election campaign for a cautious rapprochement with Russia, he never said that this would take place at the expense of relations with the West, and while cooperation with the West was originally favoured on the purely pragmatic grounds of defending Ukraine's interests, now a more 'ideological' motivation also seems to have come to the surface. In a January 1996 article on Ukraine's place in Europe, Kuchma's national security adviser, Volodymyr Horbulin, underscored the unbreakable cultural bonds between Ukraine and Europe, and claimed that in Ukrainian popular thought, integration with Europe is regarded as a necessity.[11] In June 1996 President Kuchma stated that Ukraine would like to become an associate member of the Western European Union (WEU), an aim he justified on the grounds that this would 're-establish the historical justice of the rightful return of Ukraine to Europe'.[12]

However, serious shock waves were sent through the Russian political establishment when the Ukrainian foreign minister, possibly by a slip of the tongue, mentioned at a conference on NATO in Warsaw in June 1996, organized at the initiative of the presidents of Poland, Hungary and the Czech Republic, that Ukraine could be interested in associate membership of NATO. His exact words were ' an associated status in the international organization NATO'.[13] Although his statement was partly disavowed both by officials of the foreign ministry and by the secretary of the National Security Council, Horbulin, it will be remembered in Moscow.

Russia has traditionally considered the Black Sea area a region of major interest. Russia and Turkey have fought thirteen wars against each other over the past five centuries in this region, and there is still considerable mistrust on both sides. Turkey was very unhappy with the signing in March 1995 of an agreement between Russia and Armenia for the establishment of Russian military bases in that republic, and the Turkish foreign ministry warned in May 1996 that Turkey will have to increase the number of troops along its Caucasian border unless Russia decreases its military presence in the area.[14] Russia considers influence in the Black Sea area necessary both to balance Turkish power and to exercise control in the Caucasus. It also views Turkey's political and economic support of the Crimean Tatars with scepticism, suspecting that more than just humanitarian motives lie behind this support, and that Turkey might be trying to establish a foothold in Crimea, thereby reducing Russian influence on the peninsula. The strategic importance of the Black Sea region to Russia has been further enhanced by its becoming a zone of transit for central Asian and Azerbaijani oil and gas to Europe.

Regarding the Black Sea region Russia has two central worries: that Ukraine might become an ally of Turkey against Russia, and that it might try to end the Russian military presence in Crimea. Either development would be considered a major blow to Russian influence in the region.

This partly explains Russia's insistence on keeping Sevastopol as its main base for the Black Sea Fleet, and its hostility to the construction of a new Ukrainian oil and gas terminal in Odessa. In March 1994 Turkey and Ukraine signed a joint pipeline agreement to transport Iraqi oil to Europe, either by ship through the Bosporus to Odessa, or across Turkey to the Turkish port of Samsun and from there by boat to Odessa. From Odessa it is not far to the European pipeline system.[15] The Ukrainian parliament gave the green light for the construction of the terminal in February 1995. Russia sees the project as an attempt to curb its own influence, and as an indication of a possible Ukrainian–Turkish alliance.

Ukraine's strategic priorities regarding its southern neighbours have been much less clearly defined than those regarding east-central Europe and the West. The subject has therefore not loomed large in Russian–Ukrainian relations so far, but remains of concern to Russia in the longer term.

The division of former Soviet military assets

The division of former Soviet military assets between Ukraine and Russia took place without great controversy, except in two areas: the Black Sea Fleet (BSF) and the nuclear weapons stationed on Ukrainian soil.

The Black Sea Fleet
The Black Sea Fleet was established by Catherine the Great in 1771. After several clashes with the Ottomans, Russia obtained treaty rights to base a fleet in the Black Sea in 1774. Both the BSF and Crimea itself are of great symbolic significance to many Russians. Conflict over the future of the fleet has been a perennial problem in Russian–Ukrainian relations since Ukraine's declaration of 24 August 1991 that all military hardware on its territory belonged to it. Because of the effect the issue has had on their relationship, and because of tensions between the BSF and the new Ukrainian navy (both have their headquarters in Sevastopol), both sides have emphasized the necessity of reaching an agreement. However, documents signed in June 1992, September 1993, April 1994 and June 1995 have not solved the controversy, since they were for the most part statements of intent. Three issues have dominated the controversy:

(1) The division of the vessels and aircraft This problem is the only one resolved by the documents already signed. According to the 9 June 1995 agreement, the property of the fleet is to be divided equally. However, the

final division of the vessels will be 81.7 per cent to Russia and 18.3 per cent to Ukraine. This is because some of the vessels that go to Russia will be written off against the Ukrainian debt to Russia. The practical division of vessels is now largely completed.

(2) The future bases of the two fleets Both countries want Sevastopol as their main base. Ukraine is willing to share Sevastopol, but Russia wants to rent the whole port and has suggested that Ukraine should move its own base to Donuslav. Ukraine is willing to let Russia rent Sevastopol for four or five years (by which time, according to the Ukrainians, it should be possible for Russia to establish similar facilities for the fleet on Russian territory, most likely at Novorossiisk), whereas Russia has demanded a lease of 99 years.[16] In addition, Russia wants bases in Feodosia and Kerch. Further, the price of renting Sevastopol is a contentious issue. The June 1995 agreement leaves all these issues to a permanent Russian–Ukrainian negotiating commission.[17] In July 1996 a new problem arose in connection with the adoption of the new Ukrainian constitution, which contains a general ban on foreign military bases on Ukrainian soil. However, according to presidential national security adviser Volodymyr Horbulin, this article will only come into effect after 20 years.[18]

(3) The BSF land forces (the 126th Russian Army Division) In August 1995 Ukraine and Russia signed a preliminary agreement to disband the division, and in September the Russian military newspaper *Kraznaya zvezda* reported that preparations for its dissolution were under way. However, on 6 October the Russian duma passed a bill suspending any reduction in the strength of the BSF,[19] and at the end of October a Russian foreign ministry official said that the division would not be disbanded, since it formed an integral part of the BSF.[20]

The division of the BSF is therefore still an unresolved and agonizing problem in the relationship between the two countries.

Nuclear weapons
The Ukrainian declaration of independence stated that Ukraine was to become a non-nuclear-weapon state. However, the actual disposal of arms was not all that easy to agree upon. From 1991 to 1994 the Ukrainian political leadership lingered on this issue, creating tensions both with the West and with Russia. Only in December 1994, with its accession to the Non-Proliferation Treaty (NPT), did Ukraine fully accept a non-nuclear status. At the CSCE meeting in Budapest later that month Russia

requested and obtained from Ukraine an additional note to the ratification documents, further clarifying that it acceded to the NPT treaty as a non-nuclear state. Both the Western countries and Russia were then finally satisfied with Ukrainian nuclear policy. However, though the last 200 nuclear warheads crossed the Ukrainian–Russian border on 31 May 1996, the controversy merits further examination, because it is an important element of the background to the present Ukrainian–Russian relationship. According to Russian political scientist Arkady Moshes, 'the psychological repercussions of this problem, and the dissatisfaction resulting from the concessions given during these three years, will for a long time affect the relationship between the two countries.'[21]

There were four main reasons why Ukraine lingered over this issue. First, a considerable part of the political elite thought that nuclear arms would enhance Ukrainian security *vis-à-vis* Russia. Notwithstanding the fact that Ukrainian control of the weapons was only negative – they could not launch them, only prevent them from being launched – they were considered to deter Russia from attacking or even making military threats. The former chairman of the parliament's foreign commission, Dmytro Pavlychko, claimed: ' It is like having a gun displayed on your wall. It may have no bullets but when your neighbour comes to dinner he is afraid of it.'[22] Furthermore, to take a tough stance on the nuclear issue became something of a 'test of patriotism' during the first administration.

Second, according to former Ukrainian presidential adviser Dmytro Vydrin, nuclear weapons have since their inception been invested with 'an underlying mythological image' in the Soviet Union.[23] While in the West they have served their purpose as weapons, in the Soviet Union they have been 'called upon to first serve ideological needs and only afterwards the military-political function'.[24] Because of this nuclear 'fetishism' it has been difficult for politicians in Russia and Ukraine to accept nuclear disarmament on purely rational and technical grounds.

Third, the missiles were considered to give leverage in negotiations. The fear in Kiev was that if Ukraine gave them away immediately it would not be able to obtain substantial financial assistance and security guarantees from Russia and the West.

Fourth, the existence of nuclear arms was considered to draw international attention to Ukraine. Many Ukrainian politicians feared that the world would forget about a non-nuclear Ukraine, and this would make it easier for Russia to take advantage of Ukraine.

Procrastination over the nuclear issue, combined with the absence of serious economic reform, gave Ukraine a bad international image. This put pressure on Ukrainian policy-makers and in 1993 the parliament ratified the START I treaty. In January 1994 Ukraine, Russia and the United States signed a trilateral agreement giving Ukraine security guarantees in exchange for its abandonment of its nuclear weapons. In December 1994 the Ukrainian parliament ratified the NPT treaty in the capacity of a non-nuclear country. Both former President Kravchuk and President Kuchma were instrumental in persuading the parliament to reach these decisions.

There are two main reasons why the Ukrainian parliament finally chose full nuclear disarmament. First, many of the deputies were afraid that Ukraine's increasingly negative international image might prevent the West from cooperating in other areas, and from providing financial help. Second, technical arguments convinced the deputies that most of the weapons were useless for deterrence. The SS-24s are built for a range of 9,700km, and are probably impossible to retarget for European Russia.[25] The SS-19s, with a range of about 1,000km, could be retargeted (for example) on Moscow, but to do so Ukraine would have to bypass the so-called 'black box' of security measures that is in Moscow's hands.[26] This would be hard to do technically, and would create alarm in Moscow.

Ukrainian territorial integrity

Although President Yeltsin has repeatedly acknowledged Ukrainian territorial integrity, statements by other Russian politicians and even the Russian legislature have continued to worry Ukrainian politicians.

In May 1992 the Russian Supreme Soviet declared the 1954 decision to transfer the Crimea to Ukraine illegal, and in December 1992 the Congress of People's Deputies empowered the Supreme Soviet to consider the status of Sevastopol. A summer 1994 survey of the deputies in the Russian duma revealed that only 3.4 per cent thought Crimea should belong to Ukraine.[27]

The Deputy Speaker of the Russian Supreme Soviet, Valentin Agafonov, in April 1993 sent the Crimean parliament a letter stating that he was convinced that 'no tricks or nationalistic babble can tear apart the historical blood-bonds between the peoples of Russia and Crimea'.[28] The most provocative step came on 9 July 1993, when the Supreme Soviet claimed that Sevastopol was henceforth under Russian jurisdiction. Though Yeltsin rejected these decisions – the Russian constitution giving him the right to do this – the Ukrainians were worried, since no one knew who would succeed Yeltsin.

Preparations for a wide-ranging friendship treaty have further strengthened Ukrainian suspicions that Russia will not accept Ukrainian territorial integrity. The Russian position was that it would 'respect' (*uvazhat*) the borders between the two countries, whereas the Ukrainians wanted the Russians to 'accept' (*priznat*) the borders.[29] Russia has also indicated that borders within the CIS should be regarded as only 'administrative' – guarded with only minimum control – and that the borders with non-CIS countries should be guarded by common CIS border troops. Both proposals are unacceptable to Ukraine. Though the treaty has long been ready, Yeltsin's visit to Kiev to sign it has been postponed eleven times, because no final agreement has been reached on the Black Sea Fleet issue.

B. SYSTEMIC FACTORS AND NATIONAL ATTRIBUTES

Third-country influence

Ukraine and the West

According to former presidential adviser Dmytro Vydrin, illusions concerning the West were quite widespread in the Ukrainian political leadership in the first two years of independence. A typical line of reasoning was, according to Vydrin:

> Ukraine will distance herself more and more from Russia, both in economic, political and military terms. The West will to the best of its ability help Ukraine in this, because it sees Ukraine as a buffer between itself and a potentially aggressive Russia. Further, a competition for the benevolence of Ukraine will spread among the Western powers. France will see Ukraine as an ally against possible German hegemony. Germany will see Ukraine as a partner in containing the influence of the USA and Russia. And the USA and Canada count on Ukraine as an ally in strengthening their positions in Europe.[30]

The West, however, did not live up to the expectations of many Ukrainian politicians. Western policy towards independent Ukraine developed during three stages: first, a period of neglect; second, a period of annoyance; and finally, a period of growing appreciation.

Immediately after the 1991 break-up of the Soviet Union, Western attention was very much directed towards the promising prospects of a new relationship with Russia. This, combined with a lack of knowledge about the other new states emerging from the break-up, led to the period of

71

neglect. Foreign Minister Udovenko, who was Ukrainian ambassador to the UN in 1991, said in an interview in July 1994 that he remembered how 'in the beginning I, and later together with Zlenko, ran around knocking at doors in the US State Department, and nobody wanted to talk to us.'[31] The West, and especially the USA, became aware of Ukraine when the country started to have second thoughts about getting rid of its nuclear arms. If Ukraine had chosen to retain the arms, and in addition developed operational control over them, this would have jeopardized both the NPT and the START agreements. Though Ukraine's foot-dragging on this issue caused considerable damage to its image in the West, it forced Western politicians to put Ukraine on the agenda and develop a policy towards the new state. It is possible that this would not have been done if Ukraine had quietly sent the arms to Russia, as Belarus did.

When Western politicians did look more attentively at Ukraine they saw an unstable nuclear power ruled by a team of former opposition nationalists and Communists-turned-nationalists with little or no intention of starting economic reform. This gave rise to the period of annoyance. The nuclear issue was the one of most immediate concern to Western powers, and they wanted something for nothing. A US diplomat characterized the strategy chosen by the West to achieve Ukrainian nuclear disarmament as 'to beat up on Ukraine'.[32] In Ukraine this policy seemed only to increase pro-nuclear sentiments among politicians and public alike.

Western politicians, particularly in the USA, gradually came to acknowledge that this policy towards Ukraine was counterproductive with regard to both nuclear disarmament and economic reform. There was a growing recognition that the West had a lot at stake, and that the only way to lead Ukraine onto the right track was by a carrot-and-stick policy instead of stick alone. In 1993, Strobe Talbott, US ambassador at large and special adviser to the US Secretary of State on the 'new independent states', confirmed that a major review of US Ukrainian policy had taken place. [33] He had earlier been one of the main architects behind the US plans for a 'grand strategic alliance with Russia.'[34] From the second part of 1993 it is therefore possible to talk about the development of a policy of appreciation. This was encouraged by Ukrainian divestment of nuclear weapons under Kravchuk, and gained momentum when efforts to improve relations with Russia and initiate genuine economic reform started under Kuchma. The several joint US–Ukrainian military exercises during 1995 and 1996, conducted within the framework of the Partnership for Peace programme, provide a good example of this appreciation.

There are two main approaches in the debate over what policy the West should adopt towards Ukraine. The first is that while Ukrainian independence is beneficial to the West, if the West has to choose between peace with Russia or defence of Ukrainian independence, the choice should be peace with Russia. One advocate of such a position is Eugene B. Rumer of the Rand Corporation. In an article in *Foreign Policy* on possible escalation of the conflict in Crimea and Russian intervention, he advises: 'In fashioning a response, Western policymakers must keep in mind that the key forces behind such tragic developments would be indigenous to Ukraine, not imported from Russia; that Russia has legitimate interests in that region; and that its intervention might be preferable to further instability in Ukraine'.[35] The general idea is that a resurgence of Russian imperialism within the area of the former Soviet Union would be unfortunate, but preferable to a renewal of Western–Russian confrontation.

Among Western countries, France seems at present to be most in favour of such a policy. Relations between France and Ukraine have been lukewarm since Ukraine became independent. In spring 1996 France tried, together with Russia, to block the US proposal for Ukraine to be invited to the April nuclear summit in Moscow. In the same month the Ukrainian parliamentary Speaker, Aleksandr Moroz, went on a very unsuccessful diplomatic mission to Paris. The French were, according to Moroz, only interested in when the last nuclear warheads would leave Ukraine and when the Chernobyl reactor would be closed. According to an accompanying Ukrainian journalist, Moroz in the beginning patiently, and then with increasing irritation, had to repeat 'like the Lord's Prayer' the Ukrainian position regarding the closure of Chernobyl.[36] However, the French were not interested in hearing about the financial difficulties involved in closing the power station.

The second main Western approach is that Ukrainian independence is crucial, for two reasons. If Russia accepts Ukrainian independence it will cease to be an empire; this is a necessary precondition for the development of democracy in Russia. In addition, the further the disintegration of the former Soviet Union goes in military security terms, the smaller is the security threat for the West. The most prominent advocate of this approach is former US presidential security adviser Zbigniew Brzezinski. Although he does not advocate Ukrainian membership of NATO, he does not rule it out in the longer run. While arguing that a special NATO–Ukraine treaty must not antagonize Russia, he emphasizes that such a treaty should 'include a special annex containing a joint, formal, and very explicit commitment by both parties to Ukraine's independence and security. At this stage, such a commitment need neither foreclose nor promise any future relationship between Ukraine and NATO, nor any special and truly voluntary cooperation between Russia and Ukraine.'[37] Such statements alarm not only Russian radicals but also relatively moderate Russian politicians, for example the leader of the duma's committee on international affairs, Vladimir Lukin. Lukin said in 1992 that:

> the already tense situation is aggravated by the attempts of some presumptuous circles in the Ukrainian political elite to draw a new de facto border between the West and the East – somewhere along the Don River, as the ancient Greeks did – thus remaking Ukraine into some kind of 'front line' of Western civilization. Such dreams could be regarded as naive fantasy except that they have found support among some reputable West European and US strategists, who advocate the integration of the Baltics and Ukraine into the Western community in order to counter Russia strategically.[38]

Following the change from annoyance to appreciation, the USA, and to a lesser degree the UK and Germany, have started to move in the direction of the second approach. The USA is the main force behind diplomatic initiatives regarding Ukraine in the West. A rapid rapprochement may be traced in US–Ukrainian relations since summer 1995. At the beginning of 1996 the US foreign minister Warren Christopher and the Ukrainian foreign minister Udovenko met three times in less than two months, and the State Department press secretary said: 'today there is no government [among the CIS governments] closer to us than the Ukrainian government'.[39]

Ukraine signed an agreement on partnership and cooperation with the EU in May 1994, but aside from this EU interest in Ukraine was initially scant. Economic adviser to the Ukrainian government Anders Åslund complained in 1995 that the EU's lack of interest was 'astounding'.[40] Since 1995, however, both the UK and Germany have given higher priority to their relations with Ukraine. In April 1996 the British prime minister, John Major, made an official visit to Kiev to show British support for Ukrainian independence.[41]

Alongside US and British satisfaction with Ukraine regarding its nuclear policy, initiation of economic reform and better relations with Russia, the slight readjustment of Ukraine's position regarding NATO expansion probably also facilitated the rapid US–Ukrainian rapprochement. From an initial position of scepticism towards NATO expansion, the Kuchma administration changed first to a position of neutrality and then to a position of silent approval. The only conditions for this approval are that the process is 'evolutionary', and that nuclear weapons are not stationed in the new member states.

Neither of the two Western strategies outlined advocates giving Ukraine military guarantees against Russian or other aggression. The strategies are likely to differ primarily in the level of verbal condemnation and severity of economic or other sanctions that would follow any such aggression. It is, however, likely that aggression of that kind would lead to Western reactions. A serious confrontation with Ukraine initiated by Russia is therefore likely to have negative consequences for Russian connections with the West. This is a significant cost that any Russian administration has to take into consideration.

Ukraine and central Europe

Ukraine has good relations with Poland, Slovakia, the Czech Republic and Hungary. The relationship with Hungary is especially good, because Budapest considers the 160,000 Hungarians in Zakarpattya *oblast* to be among the best-treated Hungarian minorities.[42] Some nationalists from the Czechoslovak Republican Party initially made territorial claims on Ukraine,[43] but these claims do not seem to have been taken seriously, whether in the Czech Republic, Slovakia or Ukraine. None of the central European countries, however, would be ready to enter an alliance with Ukraine to counterbalance Russia.

Among the central European countries, Poland is for political, historical and economic reasons clearly the most important to Ukraine. In autumn 1993 Ian Brzezinski, son of former US National Security Adviser Zbigniew Brzezinski and foreign policy adviser to the Ukrainian parliament, wrote an article in *Survival* entitled 'Polish–Ukrainian Relations: Europe's Neglected Strategic Axis'. His notion was that this axis was neglected by the West. However, it seems that since Ukraine became independent it has been equally neglected by Poland.

Partnership with Poland was one of the biggest hopes of the Kravchuk administration and became one of its biggest disappointments. President Kravchuk stated in the spring of 1992: 'The degree of cooperation with Poland will be higher than with any country of the CIS, including Russia.'[44] Ukrainian hopes were then kept alive by repeated encouraging statements by Polish officials, especially the president, Lech Walesa, who told a Ukrainian parliamentary delegation in December 1994: 'Without an independent Ukraine, there cannot be an independent Poland. In Poland we view our future as closer to Kiev than to New York.'[45] The Ukrainians should have learned to take Walesa's statements with a pinch of salt, however. Two days after emphasizing the uniqueness of the Polish–Ukrainian relationship to the visiting Kravchuk in Warsaw, he said that he would like 'Poland and Russia to be the pillars in Eastern Europe. Poland is ready for and wants to dance, but it takes two to tango.'[46]

The Kravchuk administration hoped that Poland would become a political and security ally and that the two countries would unite in a common fear of Russia. Likewise, Kravchuk hoped that Poland would be Ukraine's 'gateway to the West'.[47] Finally, the hope was that by allying with Poland, Ukraine would achieve a cultural and geographic redefinition, turning from the 'post-Soviet nearly-Russian' image to a central European image. None of this took place. Poland rejected Kravchuk's plan for a zone of peace and stability in central and eastern Europe, and examples of Poland serving as a gateway to the West for Ukraine are scarce. The Polish Minister of Defence, Piotr Kolodziejczyk, made clear that Poland does not equate Ukraine with the other central European countries. In an article on Poland and NATO he divided Europe into three parts: western Europe, central and eastern Europe, and 'the unstable former Soviet republics'.[48] For the Ukrainians, the clearest example of Poland ignoring Ukrainian interests was the signing in autumn 1993 of the Yamal–Frankfurt pipeline agreement between Poland and Russia. This new pipeline would seriously diminish Russian dependence on the Ukrainian pipeline system, and the Polish signature was considered as a stab in the back in Kiev.[49] Ian Brzezinski admitted in December 1994 that Polish–Ukrainian relations at present were 'in a frozen state'.[50]

Poland favours an independent Ukraine because it serves as a buffer between Poland and Russia. The election of Kuchma created considerable distress in Warsaw,[51] where leaders feared that his expected pro-Russia line would seriously weaken this buffer role. Still, the majority of Polish politicians have not considered Ukrainian independence to be so valuable as to be worth putting at risk relations with either the West or Russia. Except for a small minority of politicians, including the former defence minister Parys and the leader of the party Confederation for Independent Poland, Leszek Moczulski, who both advocate a close Polish–Ukrainian security cooperation even at the cost of Polish–Western or Polish–Russian relations, there seems to have been broad agreement in the Polish political leadership to keep a certain distance from Ukraine. However, a change may be under way in parts of the Polish political establishment. In June 1996 several former high-ranking politicians, such as former president

Walesa and former prime ministers Mazowiecki and Sukhochka, joined with prominent Ukrainian politicians such as former president Kravchuk and the leader of Rukh, Chornovil, in signing a memorandum called 'Strategic Partnership Poland–Ukraine'. Oleh Soskin, formerly – briefly – leader of the Liberal Party of Ukraine and now leader of his newly created Ukrainian National Conservative Party, was the initiator of the memorandum from the Ukrainian side. The memorandum is a statement of intent by conservative Polish and Ukrainian politicians as to the policy they would adopt if they were in government.

There were three main reasons for Poland's reluctance to foster close relations with Ukraine. First, there was a fear that obligations to and treaties with Ukraine might hinder Polish integration into NATO and the EU. Second, there was a fear of angering Russia, which could both endanger Polish security and work against the chances for democracy in Russia. Yeltsin's former political adviser, Sergei Stankevich, warned Polish officials during a visit to Warsaw in May 1993 that Ukraine and Belarus fell within Russia's sphere of influence, and that close military ties between Poland and these countries would be viewed very negatively by Moscow. The Polish foreign minister, Andrzej Olechowski, therefore said in December 1993: 'Poland must not do anything that would make it more difficult for Russia to become democratic and friendly toward our country.'[52] Third, Poland was afraid of being dragged into conflicts between Russia and Ukraine that do not concern Polish interests, such as the Crimean question.

Poland – and, for that matter Hungary and Slovakia – have therefore so far not been allies on which Ukraine could count to balance against Russia. The three reasons for Polish reluctance are still influential in Warsaw, but developments such as the Polish–Ukrainian memorandum indicate a change of perception in parts of the Polish political establishment. It is also noteworthy that President Kuchma, after a meeting with his Polish counterpart, Kwasniewski, in June 1996, stated: 'I am glad that we could agree on all questions, including the questions related to European security.'[53]

Ukraine and its southern neighbours
Romania is the only country besides Russia to make territorial claims on Ukraine. In 1940, as a result of the Molotov–Ribbentrop Pact, the Red Army moved into Romania and annexed several territories to the Soviet Union: northern Bukovyna, the northernmost part of Bessarabia and the Hertsa area (these areas now constitute the Chernivtsi *oblast*); southern

Bessarabia (now the southernmost part of Odessa *oblast*); and the little Serpent Island just off both countries' Black Sea coast, reported to contain rich oil and gas deposits.[54] On 24 June 1991 the Romanian parliament condemned the annexation, and in November the Romanian government and parliament both protested against the former Romanian territories' participation in the Ukrainian independence referendum. Several rounds of negotiations between the two countries in autumn 1995 failed to resolve the border issues and on 31 October a Ukrainian foreign ministry official said no further meetings were planned.[55] In December 1995 the Romanian foreign minister, Teodor Meleshkanu, announced that Romania would take the dispute over the Serpent Island to the International Court of Justice in The Hague if no agreement could be reached with Ukraine.[56]

Romania is not likely in the foreseeable future to advance military threats against the much stronger Ukraine in order to regain these lost territories, but the possibility of conflict escalation cannot be ruled out. Nationalist sentiments seem to be on the rise in Romania. If Ukraine gets tangled in a conflict with Russia or in domestic turmoil, and there is at the same time a nationalist government in power in Bucharest, such a government could feel tempted to take advantage of the situation. Thus, depending on political developments in Romania, an additional security concern for Ukraine could arise that could increase the costs of a military dispute with Russia.

At present, however, relations between Ukraine and Romania are peaceful. In 1996 both countries decided to shift the focus of their relations from politics to economics. Trade between the two countries is on the rise, and the two chairmen of a Ukrainian–Romanian coordinating committee established in 1996 agreed that increased economic cooperation would undoubtedly increase the chances of later political agreement. Paradoxically, the claims to northern Bukovina and Bessarabia seem to be doing more damage to Romania's relations with Russia than with Ukraine. Russia and Romania have been negotiating a friendship treaty since 1992, but have so far not been able to reach agreement. The main issue seems to be Romania's insistence that an article condemning the annexation of Bessarabia and northern Bukovyna be included in the treaty, which Russia rejects.[57]

Ukraine's relations with Moldova are basically good, Ukraine considering Moldova to be an ally in the context of CIS cooperation. This is despite the fact that the part of Moldova east of the river Dniestr, which in 1991 proclaimed itself the independent republic of Pridnyestrovya, was until 1940 part of the Ukrainian Soviet Socialist Republic. Some Ukrainians still regard these areas as belonging to Ukraine. In an article in the official journal of the Ukrainian foreign ministry, *Polityka i Chas* (Politics and Time) in 1992, the Ukrainian historian V. Boechko set out to prove the constant settlement and domination of Ukrainians in the present Chernivtsi *oblast*, southern Bessarabia and Pridnyestrovya. He refers to Pridnyestrovya as 'ancient Ukrainian lands'.[58]

When Pridnyestrovya declared itself independent on 25 August 1991, and later became engaged in armed conflict with the Moldovan authorities over independence, there were both historical and ethnic reasons for Ukraine to support the secessionists, and considerable support for them among Ukrainian nationalists. One of Rukh's leaders, A. Lavrinovych, was hailed at a conference of Ukrainians in Pridnyestrovya in March 1993 for saying that Pridnyestrovya 'should never be a part of Moldova, and certainly not of Romania'.[59] The Ukrainian authorities, on the other hand, while remaining neutral, sympathized with Moldova in the conflict. In 1992 President Kravchuk sent the Ukrainian National Guard to the border – not to support the secessionists, but to prevent the fighting from spreading into Ukraine. Ukraine and Moldova have since developed a close relationship, involving the exchange of intelligence, training of Moldovan officers, and cooperation between Moldovan and Ukrainian border troops.[60]

There are four main reasons why Ukraine chose the Moldovan side in the secession issue. First, supporting the secessionists might have led to renewed fighting that could have spilled over into Ukrainian territory. Furthermore, any renewal of the conflict is likely to send thousands of refugees into Ukraine. The former chief of the Ukrainian general staff, Anatoliy Lopata, said in August 1994 that under no circumstance should Ukraine get involved in the Pridnyestrovia conflict.[61] Second, if Ukraine claimed Pridnyestrovya as Ukrainian, that would both lend force to Romania's claim on Chernivtsi and southern Bessarabia and further encourage Crimea's separatists. Third, continued hostilities in Pridnyestrovya would be a pretext for Russia to retain the 8,000-strong 14th Army there to protect the Russian population; and the presence of this and other pro-Russian military units on Ukraine's southwestern border might force Ukraine to fight on two fronts in the event of an armed conflict with Russia. Fourth, the leadership of the secessionist movement includes many pro-Russian orthodox Communists. It is not in Ukraine's interest to support them.

A conflict between Moldova and Ukraine over Pridnyestrovya is therefore highly unlikely. In 1996 Ukraine instead launched several initiatives to try to negotiate between the two sides. However, if a lasting peace settlement is not reached and the 14th Army remains, or if new hostilities break out and the Russian military presence is enlarged, this is likely to strain relations between Ukraine and Russia further. Moldova and Russia signed an agreement on troop withdrawal in October 1994, but the Russian duma did not ratify it. By early 1997 there were few prospects of an early withdrawal of troops.[62]

Economic relations and politics

Economic relations can influence interstate relations in several ways. If one country is dependent on another for a specific strategic commodity, and it believes or suspects that the other country might try to use its possession of this commodity to extort unfair economic or political concessions, such economic dependence can have a deleterious influence on the relationship. If, on the other hand, two countries see possibilities for mutually profitable economic cooperation, then such cooperation can have a beneficial effect in the political realm. Those engaged in the sectors of the economy profiting from the cooperation might put pressure on their authorities to pursue good political relations with the other country, and successful negotiations of economic agreements might increase trust between the two countries. In Ukrainian–Russian relations both tendencies are present.

The economic structures Ukraine inherited from the Soviet Union were highly interwoven with other post-Soviet states. For example, 80 per cent of Ukraine's industrial production did not constitute a complete technological cycle inside the country's borders.[63] The majority of the items needed for industrial production came from Russia, so that before 1991, 70 per cent of Ukrainian imports came from Russia .[64] That figure had decreased to 50 per cent in 1996.[65] Ukraine depends upon Russia for deliveries of oil and gas, and Russia depends upon Ukraine for its exports of oil and gas to western and central Europe, since the Ukrainian pipeline system carries 90 per cent of Russian gas exports.[66] Russia is also dependent upon Ukraine for imports of various types of metal and of several crucial items for its gas, oil and mining industries, and upon the Ukrainian market for the sale of oil, gas and non-ferrous metals.

The mutual dependence in the energy sector can be used for political purposes by both sides, but mostly by Russia. Ukraine could, if forced into a corner, sabotage the Russian oil and gas exports to the West; this would be a fairly radical step, however, and is not really a practical political tool until and unless a serious conflict erupts with Russia. In addition, Ukraine has accumulated a considerable debt for oil and gas it has received but not paid for. Russia, on the other hand, has a more convenient and flexible foreign policy tool in temporarily stopping or limiting the supplies, and demanding payment of the debt. According to one observer, as soon as Russia discovered that Kuchma was not Russia's man, it immediately cut back on the deliveries of oil and gas.[67] Volodymyr Pylypchuk, the chairman of the Ukrainian parliamentary commission on economic reform, complained that the Russian 'oil whip' negates the development of a sovereign Ukrainian state.[68]

However, Russia's opportunities to use gas deliveries as a political tool against Ukraine are also limited. Russia cannot cut deliveries to Ukraine totally without also stopping deliveries to western Europe. For both political and economic reasons this is something it would be very reluctant to do. It might also be dangerous only to reduce gas deliveries to Ukraine, since a certain pressure in the pipelines is necessary to avoid the danger of explosion.[69] The planned pipeline through Belarus and Poland is therefore of particular importance. According to a 1995 analysis of geopolitical changes in Europe published by the Russian Academy of Sciences' Europe Institute, this new pipeline would 'strongly enhance Russia's possibilities in its dialogue with Ukraine'.[70]

In addition to the threat of suspension of deliveries, the Ukrainian debt to Russia for oil and gas supplied, which has risen steadily since independence, has further weakened the Ukrainian position in negotiations. In summer 1993 Russia tried to get Kravchuk to give up Ukraine's share of the Black Sea Fleet in return for a reduction in the debt, and in 1994 the Russian oil and gas company Gazprom wanted to take over parts of the Ukrainian pipeline system in exchange for debt reductions. However, according to the then Ukrainian prime minister, Marchuk, in 1995 Ukraine for the first time managed to meet its debt obligations in full – although that was only possible because Russia was willing to renegotiate the Ukrainian loans under Western pressure, and because Ukraine could use IMF credits to pay for the loans.

To extricate itself from this awkward situation, Ukraine is trying to reduce its dependence on Russian oil and gas deliveries. At least three ways of doing this have been tried: seeking alternative suppliers; exploiting domestic reserves; and commercializing larger parts of the oil and gas trade.

From the moment of independence Ukraine has tried to find alternative suppliers of oil and gas. The above-mentioned pipeline agreement with Turkey is one example. Separate agreements have also been signed with Iran, Turkmenistan, Tatarstan and Bashkortostan. The Ukrainian authorities have also tried to bypass Moscow by signing direct agreements with the oil-producing Tyumen *oblast* in Russia. This has been possible in part because many ethnic Ukrainians work there. The trade is based on barter deals whereby Ukraine sends food in exchange for oil and gas. Buying oil in the Middle East (Iran, Iraq) and Azerbaijan has so far been difficult owing to lack of pipeline and storage facilities.

Ukraine has sizeable gas reserves, and pins high hopes on the indications of substantial gas and oil deposits on the continental shelf off Crimea and in the Odessa area. However, it is a long way from proving the existence of reserves to actual production. Exploitation of own reserves is therefore only going to reduce the dependence on Russian deliveries to a very limited extent in the short term.

The more oil and gas trade is run through private companies, the less occurs as a direct state-to-state transaction between Ukraine and Russia. Commercialization therefore reduces the opportunity for Russian authorities to use oil and gas deliveries as a political weapon. According to the former Ukrainian presidential adviser, Dmytro Vydrin, this commercialization is already well under way.[71]

Oil and gas trade remains a stumbling-block for improved relations between Ukraine and Russia. Russia is eager to be paid, and suspects that Ukraine is simply testing out Russia's goodwill, while Ukraine is accusing Russia of exploiting Ukraine's weak energy position for political purposes.

With Ukrainian–Russian trade rapidly decreasing in the first years after independence, and the Kravchuk administration showing scant interest in reversing that trend, the prospects were meagre for economic cooperation and trade to become a stabilizing factor in Ukrainian–Russian relations. However, with the advent of the Kuchma administration, efforts were made to revive economic relations. After July 1994 Ukraine became a promoter of economic cooperation in the CIS, and in February 1995 it signed a bilateral free trade agreement with Russia. In January 1995 the establishment of so-called financial-industrial conglomerates (FICs) was sanctioned by a presidential decree. FICs are large industrial companies established with joint Ukrainian–Russian capital. Several such groups have already been established, and according to Dmytro Vydrin a sufficient number of them will create an 'economic self-interest in peace' that will be difficult for any politician to ignore.[72] On the other hand, it should be noted that there is also a substantial fear in Ukraine of too much Russian involvement in Ukrainian enterprises. Mykola Honchar of the Ukrainian National Institute for Strategic Studies has warned against aggressive Russian businessmen, 'for whom the slogan of a greater Russia is not an empty phrase'.[73]

The new line in foreign economic policy already seems to have yielded some results for Ukraine. Since June 1995 its exports to Russia have steadily increased at the same time as imports from Russia have fallen. Of particular importance to a country such as Ukraine, with a large farming sector, is that 25 per cent of exports to Russia consists of agricultural products.[74]

However, with non-energy trade, as with oil and gas, there is a feeling on the Ukrainian side that Russia is exploiting the situation. After the signing of the free trade agreement in February 1995 both countries established expert groups to work out the details of the agreement. According to the Ukrainian side only Ukraine took this task seriously, and when the then prime minister, Marchuk, went to Moscow to try to speed up the process, he was told by the Russian prime minister, Chernomyrdin, to enter the customs union instead.[75] The treaty on a customs union was signed by Russia, Belarus and Kazakstan in January 1995, while Ukraine chose to remain outside, fearing Russian dominance in the union. There is a feeling in Ukraine that Russia will exert whatever leverage is available in the non-energy sector as well, to press Ukraine towards closer integration.

Non-energy economic relations between Ukraine and Russia therefore have a mixed impact upon the relationship between the two countries. On the one hand, increased trade since mid-1995, the emergence of a mixed business community with vested interests in business not being interrupted by worsened political relations between the two countries, and Ukraine's new interest in expanding economic cooperation within the CIS are all factors that have a stabilizing effect on the relationship. On the other hand, Ukraine's constant fear of Russian attempts to undermine its independence, either by trying to coerce Ukraine into economic communities it does not want to join, or by means of 'imperial businessmen' buying up Ukrainian enterprises, and Russia's impatience with what it sees as half-heartedness towards economic integration, both contribute to continued mistrust between the countries.

Relative military capabilities

According to Sherman Garnett, an expert on post-Soviet affairs, 'the favourite downside scenario of many in the West – war between Russia and Ukraine – will be beyond the capabilities of both sides for years to come.'[76] Neither side will feel it has sufficient domestic political coherence and military strength to engage the other in an armed conflict.

The 24 August 1991 decision by the Ukrainian parliament 'On Military Formations in Ukraine' – only two days after the abortive Moscow coup – initiated a process that eventually cut short all Moscow's attempts at preserving a unified military structure. Since Ukraine inherited as much as 40 per cent of the former Soviet armed forces – 1.2 million soldiers and their equipment[77] – Moscow's attempts at creating CIS joint armed forces came to nothing. Although Ukraine became rich in personnel and armaments, this did not mean that Ukraine also suddenly became a mighty military power: to make the armed forces fit Ukrainian security needs, large-scale reorganization, retraining, relocation and reduction of personnel were necessary.

Military legislation accordingly developed on a rapid scale during 1992. Three categories of legislation were necessary: for transfer of command; to establish a social safety net for personnel during the transition period; and for the everyday operation of the forces.[78] The new armed forces were to be established on the basis of the Odessa, Kiev and Carpathian military districts, totalling between 400,000 and 420,000 troops, consisting of an army, a navy and an air force, and all servicemen were to be required to pledge an oath of loyalty to Ukraine. Despite contradicting orders being issued by the former Soviet defence ministry, Ukrainization of personnel and equipment took place rapidly and with only very minor confrontations.

The army

The total number of troops in the army is expected to be cut to 400,000 by 1997 and finally to about 200,000 between 1997 and 2000.[79] The end result aimed at by the programme 'Army 2000' is: five motorized infantry divisions, one tank division, seven motorized infantry brigades, three tank brigades, two airborne brigades and several supply units. The purpose of the reorganization, besides the reduction in troops, is to increase mobility and manoeuvrability, while retaining defensive fire-power.[80]

Army *matériel* has also been significantly reduced. By October 1995 the Ukrainian army had 5,050 armed combat vehicles (ACVs), 4,080 tanks and 4,040 artillery units.[81]

The air force

With an inheritance of 1,380 warplanes, Ukraine in 1991 had the third largest air force in the world. Lack of resources to keep and operate such a 'fleet', the calculation that so many planes are not necessary to defend Ukraine, and restrictions under Convential Forces in Europe (CFE) agreements, have made Ukraine also decide to cut its air force capabilities substantially. By October 1995 the Ukrainian air force had 1,090 combat planes and 330 helicopters.[82] The number of troops in the air force will be reduced from 86,000 to 25,000, and the number of planes eventually to 590.[83]

In the Soviet period the air force was divided into the Air Force (tasked with supporting ground forces at the front), and the Air Defence Force (tasked with the defence of strategically important domestic entities: nuclear missiles, power plants, big cities, etc.). In the new Ukrainian air force these elements are merged. However, this has so far only taken place on paper. There is as yet no common command, and technical and organizational amalgamation is time-consuming and costly.

The navy

The December 1991 law on the armed forces also stipulated the creation of a Ukrainian navy from the Ukrainian share of the Black Sea Fleet. Since the negotiations on the division of the fleet have dragged on for five years, and no conclusive agreement has been reached, the Ukrainian navy remains an embryonic state. In January 1992 the Ukrainian defence minister, commenting on the Ukrainian military doctrine, described the Ukrainian navy as basically a coastal force that would consists of four brigades, a naval aviation division, air defence units and two helicopter squadrons.[84]

The doctrine

The Ukrainian military doctrine was adopted by parliament in October 1993. Two aspects are of particular political importance. The first is that the doctrine does not identify any country or block of countries as potential enemies; the second is that it prohibits the use of the armed forces in the case of domestic disturbances. The main part of the document is devoted to a description of what kind of armed forces Ukraine is planning to build, and in this respect the doctrine, according to one observer, resembles the Russian one in giving 'a brief acknowledgement that money is tight, followed by a shopping list reminiscent of the Soviet era spending spree.'[85]

An assessment of capabilities

Three factors will greatly influence the armed forces' efficiency in a combat situation: the quantity and quality of arms and troops, the combat readiness of the troops, and the deployment of the forces.

During the Cold War, the forces stationed on Ukrainian soil constituted the second echelon of the Warsaw Pact forces. Because of this they were given high priority in the Red Army. The quality of the equipment is contested, however. Russian military representatives say it is some of the best, but Ukrainian officials say a lot of it is outdated. There is, however, little reason to doubt that the amount and to some degree the quality of the military hardware inherited by Ukraine is sufficient to deter Russia.

Ukrainian authorities cannot be sure of their troops' willingness to fight Russia. According to Hryhorii Omelchenko, a member of the defence ministry's Higher Attestation Commission, in 1991 some 90 per cent of the higher officers and some 70 per cent of all general officer ranks were non-Ukrainians, predominantly Russians.[86] As mentioned earlier, unofficial surveys indicate that a majority of the officers would not fight if Russia were the enemy.[87] Though a process of Ukrainization of the military ranks began in June 1992, the creation of a cohesive and motivated Ukrainian military will take time. A survey among Ukrainian officers in June 1996 revealed that 37 per cent would not be against the formation of a Russia–Belarus–Ukraine military block.[88]

The troops are poorly trained, especially the air force, because of lack of fuel and other resources. In addition, daunting social problems, especially the lack of housing for officers and the ritual bullying by older recruits (*didovshchina*), has lowered troop morale. In the first half of 1994 alone, 74 soldiers committed suicide. In 1993, every tenth officer turned to the state Committee for Social Security of Armed Personnel for financial assistance.[89] In the June 1996 survey quoted above, 73 per cent of the respondents said that unlawful sale of military equipment is one of the most important problems of the Ukrainian armed forces today, and an astounding 57 per cent thought the armed forces would not be able to defend the country if attacked.[90] One might wonder, however, whether this view is as much a way of expressing despair over the situation of servicemen as a realistic evaluation of combat ability.

The forces Ukraine inherited were largely located in the western and southern regions. Though the most likely threat to Ukrainian security is located in the northeast, that deployment pattern has not been changed. This is probably not only because of the financial expenses of redeployment. According to Stepan Oliynik, military adviser to the Ukrainian parliament: 'For political reasons there are no operative commands in Eastern Ukraine'.[91] Absence of any serious redeployment reduces Ukraine's ability to respond to Russian aggression at an early stage.

Russian troops might also be reluctant to fight Ukraine. The Russian army would probably find Ukraine more worth fighting for than Chechenia, since Ukraine is likely to be considered more a natural part of Russia than Chechenia by a majority of Russian troops. On the other hand, the mere idea of fighting the Ukrainians, considered by many Russians to be almost the same people as themselves, is very alien. Most Russian families have relatives in Ukraine and there are a myriad other ties that bind the two countries together. It is therefore uncertain what the Russian troops would do and what their fighting morale would be if they were told to go to war against Ukraine.

Though Russia is the stronger militarily, Ukraine is sufficiently strong to discourage most military adventures. Few politicians in Ukraine, therefore, fear a direct military attack on the country. First deputy foreign minister Boris Tarasyuk confidently stated in July 1995: 'There is currently no country or group of countries that could dare attack Ukraine militarily.'[92]

Other factors

The first additional point to note is that, for both Ukrainians and Russians, nationalists and moderates, a certain level of patriotism in both statements and deeds is necessary to maintain domestic political credibility. These demands are of course stronger for the nationalists on both sides than for the moderates. The extent of the demand for a display of patriotism, however, and the degree to which it influences foreign policy, are changing. Foreign policy statements are often bold before elections, since they contain messages for the domestic audience as well as for other countries. This means that politicians might advocate more robust policies in public than the deals they suggest to their opponents in negotiations. However, the discrepancy between words and deeds cannot be allowed to grow too wide, since this will lead to a loss of credibility.

Second, the policy-making process itself may influence the outcome in a way not planned at the outset by the political leadership. This has, for example, been a perennial problem of Russian foreign policy.[93] Several uncoordinated actors all implementing foreign policy can often distort an originally coherent plan.

Third, a policy outcome may also be influenced by characteristics of

87

the individuals engaged in negotiations. For example, the good personal contacts of former Ukrainian presidential adviser Dmytro Vydrin in the Russian political elite seemed to be instrumental in improving relations between Russia and Ukraine during 1994–5.[94] On the other hand, the fact that the Russian delegations in negotiations with Ukraine were often led by Yuriy Dubinin might have been a major hindrance in attempts to reach a compromise.[95] Most major breakthroughs were made when Dubinin for one reason or another was absent from the negotiations.

C. SCENARIOS FOR THE EVOLVING RELATIONSHIP

Having summarized the problems of Ukrainian–Russian relations, and keeping in mind the most important systemic conditions and national attributes that influence these relations, I will now discuss the future of Russian–Ukrainian relations by considering scenarios constructed from four possible combinations of political leaderships in Russia and Ukraine:

(1) Nationalists in Ukraine and nationalists in Russia.
(2) Nationalists in Ukraine and moderates in Russia.
(3) Moderates in Ukraine and nationalists in Russia.
(4) Moderates in Ukraine and moderates in Russia.

The labels *nationalist* and *moderate* are to be understood only as related to Ukrainian–Russian relations. Of course, nationalism and moderation come in degrees, but for the sake of simplicity I have treated both variables as fixed attributes. *Ukrainian moderates* are in this connection those who think that it is quite possible for independent Ukraine to live peacefully with Russia, and who base their policy mostly on pragmatic arguments. *Ukrainian nationalists,* on the other hand, are those who think that although good relations with Russia are worth striving for, history has shown that this is extremely difficult for Ukraine to achieve. Because of Russia's inherent imperialism and its doubtful European character, Ukraine should integrate as much as possible with the West and with central Europe. This, they believe, would help revive the Ukrainian economy, enhance Ukrainian security, and entrench Ukraine's European identity. They therefore take a negative stance on most kinds of cooperation with Russia.

Russian moderates are in this connection those who may not like, but nevertheless accept, the idea of an independent Ukraine. Most of them are in favour of close integration, but they will refrain from forcing this integration through. *Russian nationalists,* on the other hand, do not accept the idea of Ukrainian independence. They consider most means to achieve integration justifiable, including, in the last instance, military force.

I find it useful in discussing the four scenarios to use some conditions presented by the political scientist Michael Brecher in considering the initiation of military disputes.[96] He describes three perceptual attributes – *high value threat* (or *high value loss,* depending on the context), *time pressure* and *heightened war likelihood* – and one systemic attribute – *disruptive interaction* – as necessary conditions for a government to consider the use of armed force. If one accepts Brecher's attributes, the chances that Ukraine and Russia will end up in military dispute with each other will depend upon the degree of value threat, time pressure and war likelihood felt by the parties, and the level of disruptive interaction between them.

Scenario one: nationalists in Ukraine and nationalists in Russia

Likelihood of the scenario

Yeltsin's victory in the 1996 Russian presidential elections was a relief for Ukraine. His moderate policy towards Ukraine is now the line most likely to be followed by Russia in the coming years. However, from the Ukrainian leadership's point of view, a nationalist takeover later, or the adoption of a more nationalist stance by the present regime in Moscow, cannot be ruled out. Nobody knows what political forces will be at the forefront of Russian politics in five years' time. There is an audience for nationalist slogans in the Russian population, and the Russian sociologist Igor Kliamkin, who has conducted several surveys on Russian attitudes towards Ukrainian independence, has come up with unambiguous results: 'The citizens of Russia cannot accept Ukraine as an independent state, no longer a part of Russia.'[97] There is also considerable insecurity regarding the fate of the Yeltsin government; factors such as Yeltsin's health and the rising influence of Aleksandr Lebed are watched closely in Kiev – especially as Lebed said in October 1995 that 'the reunion of the former Soviet republics will become a reality in the near future'.[98] Thus the likelihood of a nationalist takeover in Moscow cannot be ruled out.

In the 1994 parliamentary and presidential elections in Ukraine, nationalism and anti-Russian slogans did not gather much popular support. Support for the nationalists is still largely confined to western and parts of central Ukraine. To win elections in Ukraine, politicians should advocate cooperation with, rather than distance from, Russia. This climate is also likely to prevail because the basically pro-cooperation population of eastern and southern Ukraine, large parts of the population of central Ukraine and the population of Crimea together constitute a clear majority of the population.

Thus, a nationalist government in Ukraine is not very likely. However, in the event of the emergence of a strongly imperialist mood in Moscow, initially moderate Ukrainian politicians could become more nationalist. Although large parts of the population might not support them, there may be increased backing for the nationalists in regions or social classes where they had previously raised little enthusiasm. According to a Ukrainian observer, Stepan Romanchuk, a process of 'patriotization' at the elite level has already started. A considerable number of Communists, socialists and pragmatic economic reformers in the parliament, expected to be proponents of closer relations with Russia, have become increasingly concerned with the defence of Ukrainian independence.[99] That does not necessarily mean that they have become nationalists, but it does indicate that they might support nationalist positions in policy towards Russia if external pressure were to increase sufficiently. The scenario is therefore likely enough to be worth considering.

Possible spurs for conflict escalation

(1) Russia and Ukrainian independence The separation of Ukraine from Russia as a result of the collapse of the Soviet Union was one of the hardest blows for many Russian nationalists to take. The loss of political influence in a strategic area for Russia was important, but there was much more to it than that. Kiev is often considered in Russia as the mother of Russian cities. The prominent Russian nationalist, Sergey Baburin, has said: 'Little Russia [Ukraine] is the centre of old Russia. Compared to Kiev, Russia is a periphery. This is because Russia is the result of the expansion of one united Slavic state.'[100] Not only is Ukrainian independence a great value loss for Russia, it is also considered unnatural and against history. When the nationalist chairman of the Russian duma committee on CIS affairs, Konstantin Zatulin, was commenting on the question of Ukrainian territorial integrity, he answered by denouncing 'the never before in history existing borders of a never before in history existing state'.[101]

Russian nationalists generally consider Ukrainian independence as a kind of betrayal not only of Russia but of the people of Ukraine. They consider the collapse of the Soviet Union in 1991 to be the result of a combination of Gorbachev's failed policy and the activities of small nationalist cliques in each republic. They feel that if these nationalist elites, driven by a selfish greed for power, hinder the realization of the desire for reintegration among the Ukrainian masses, then not even the use of arms by Russia should be excluded to thwart these efforts.

For the Ukrainian nationalists the value threat of losing independence is as strong as, or even stronger than, the loss of Ukraine for the Russian nationalists, and the survival of Ukrainian independence is the supreme goal. It is a goal in itself and not just a means of securing the population's well-being.

Judging from statements by many Russian nationalists, they are not, at least in the short run, going to feel much time pressure for getting Ukraine back. Most Russian nationalists are convinced that the reunification process will occur naturally: that is, the Ukrainians will come back by themselves as the Belorussians have done.

A feeling of time pressure might evolve, however, in the longer term. The Russian nationalists might get tired of waiting, and a feeling might spread among them that this 'independence prank' had lasted long enough. Moreover, if the Ukrainian economy starts to recover, and the nation consolidates around a common national idea, this may lead the Russian nationalists to doubt whether Ukraine will come back by itself after all. It will then become important to integrate Kiev as soon as possible, since the more consolidated and economically prosperous Ukraine becomes, the more difficult it will be to reclaim.

On the Ukrainian nationalist side the feeling of time pressure is stronger. In security terms, Ukrainian nationalists consider Russia to be a perpetual threat. This is the most fundamental lesson of Ukrainian history. Naturally Ukraine should try to achieve peaceful relations with Moscow, but that cannot be an alternative to full integration into west and central European security structures.

Ukrainian nationalists are also very concerned about the cultural aspects of the relationship. They firmly believe that Ukraine is a European country, both geographically and culturally, whereas Russia is Asian or half-Asian. According to Yurii Kostenko, the former Ukrainian chief negotiator with Russia on questions of nuclear arms, 'Ukraine is a purely European state, Russia is Euro-Asian.'[102] Dmytro Pavlychko, in outlining the direction of Ukrainian foreign policy, stated: 'The integration into the general European structures will move us to Europe … where we were born and grew up as a nation. From here we were torn away and forced into Asiatic imprisonment, dressed in the cloak of Moscow, and trained in the Slavic-Russian language by the great-grandchildren of Genghis Khan.'[103] The closer the relationship is with Russia, the more 'Asianized' Ukraine will become. The Ukrainian nationalists feel that the longer it takes for Ukraine to distance itself from Russia, politically and economically, the smaller are the chances that it will succeed. They therefore have a strong feeling of time pressure. The present period of Russian weakness is the one golden opportunity that Ukraine can exploit to 'go to Europe'. The more Russia recovers, economically and militarily, the smaller are the chances for a Europeanized, independent Ukraine.

Disruptive interaction is almost guaranteed under this scenario, at least at the verbal level. It is sufficient to cite some leading Russian nationalists on, for example, the willingness to use force for the purpose of reunification. Sergey Baburin has stated: 'Either Ukraine reunites with Russia, or there will be war.'[104] A spokesman for the main umbrella organization of Russian nationalists until 1993, the National Salvation Front, was more subtle. He said that although the Front would not be in favour of immediately sending the Tamar division against Kiev, it would ultimately be ready to use any means necessary to ensure the re-establishment of a unified state.[105]

(2) Foreign policy decisions A nationalist Ukrainian leadership would try to connect Ukraine to west and central European security structures. If Ukraine tried to become a member of NATO, this would provide both a sense of time pressure and a feeling of heightened war likelihood among Russian nationalists. Both conditions, otherwise lacking, would then be present. Preventing Ukraine from entering such alliances could be a matter of urgency and create time pressure. West and central European countries are not ready to enter any anti-Russia coalition with Ukraine. But, if the scattered calls in the West for more attention to be given to the non-Russian republics of the former Soviet Union, to preserve what Zbigniew Brzezinski has called 'geostrategical pluralism,' coalesce into a clear strategy, including talk about Ukrainian membership of NATO, the feeling of time pressure among the Russian nationalists would grow enormously.

(3) Ukrainian territorial integrity Russian nationalists consider the loss of eastern and southern Ukraine as a serious value loss, but probably not as serious as the loss of Crimea. The then Russian Vice-President, Aleksandr Rutskoi, stated in August 1992 that 'the Crimea was Russian, it's covered with Russian blood, and it must be Russia's.'[106] As with the acceptance of Ukrainian independence, there will be not be not much time pressure, however, since it is believed that both Crimea and eastern and

southern Ukraine will come back, either alone or with Ukraine as a whole. One nationalist Russian general said in 1992: 'Ukraine or rather Eastern Ukraine will come back in five, ten or fifteen years. Western Ukraine can go to hell.'[107] There is likely to be disruptive interaction in connection with these areas. Russian nationalists are likely to feel free to promote their political influence and even engage in local politics in these areas (as in Zatulin's involvement in Crimean affairs). A serious increase in disruptive interaction and time pressure, however, is probable only under two conditions.

The first condition is extensive attempts at Ukrainianization in eastern and southern Ukraine by Ukrainian nationalists. This is not likely. Though the Ukrainian nationalists would undoubtedly like the population in these areas to be more 'Ukrainian', they are not likely to start any campaign of Ukrainianization. As explained in Chapter 3, most Ukrainian nationalists have a fairly liberal attitude when it comes to minority policy.

The second condition is a significant growth in the strength of separatist demands in eastern and southern Ukraine. This is most likely to happen in the event of significantly better economic development in Russia than in Ukraine. Any Ukrainian authorities are likely to thwart separatist efforts in these areas, and any such actions by the Ukrainian authorities are likely to be strongly condemned by Russian nationalists.

Similarly, if Crimea were reunited with Russia it would be an unacceptable loss for the Ukrainian nationalists. However, a nationalist Russian government would probably not feel the same time pressure with regard to the eventual status of the Crimea as it would feel if Ukraine were to turn against Russia and join military coalitions to the west. In much the same way as with the question of accepting Ukrainian independence, there would be a feeling that Crimea, either together with or slightly ahead of Ukraine, would eventually come back under Russian control. Though the status of Crimea would definitely be a sensitive issue under this scenario, it would not in itself lead to high time pressure on the Russian nationalist side.

(4) The Black Sea Fleet For Ukrainian nationalists, the prospect of the Russian Black Sea Fleet continuing to be based in Ukraine, occupying the base of Sevastopol, is an intolerable value threat. Similarly, the expulsion of the Fleet, and thereby the termination of more than 200 years of Russian military domination in Crimea, would be an intolerable value loss for Russian nationalists. In August 1995 Vitaliy Zhuravlev, leader of the Russian duma sub-committee for Slavic peoples, called Crimea 'the

geopolitical vanguard of the whole Slavic world'.[108] A nationalist Ukrainian government could consider an expulsion of all Russian military units from Crimea a limited and perfectly legitimate action to secure full control over its own territory. Russian nationalists, on the other hand, would probably interpret such an action as almost tantamount to a declaration of war. It would therefore be a matter of urgency for Russia to act before the expulsion to prevent it, in order not to lose tactical advantages in a possible battle. All four preconditions for initiating a dispute would be present. This line of development is also somewhat more likely than the previous one. The Ukrainians would not regard an expulsion as a declaration of war. It would therefore demand less courage to execute, and the decision would not directly depend on external support. If Scenario one should emerge, the Russian military presence in Crimea would be one of the most contentious issues.

Scenario two: nationalists in Ukraine and moderates in Russia

I do not find this scenario sufficiently probable to address. With a moderate Russian leadership and fairly stable relations between the two countries, Ukrainian nationalists are unlikely to achieve power in the foreseeable future. One could imagine a non-constitutional takeover by the military in a domestic crisis situation. However, as argued in Chapter 2, this is not very likely, and there is no reason to believe that a possible military regime would be much more nationalist than a civil one. Neither the Ukrainian troops nor the majority of the upper echelons of the army are any more anti-Russian in foreign policy than the rest of the population.[109]

Scenario three: moderates in Ukraine and nationalists in Russia

Likelihood of the scenario
This is a fairly likely scenario. As already mentioned, a nationalist government is possible in Russia, but such a government would not necessarily frighten the Ukrainians into becoming nationalist. There is good reason to believe that the majority electorate – in eastern, southern and parts of central Ukraine – is not going to see Ukrainian nationalism as the answer to nationalism in Russia.

Possible spurs for conflict escalation
(1) Russia and Ukrainian independence What would distinguish this scenario from Scenario one is that, in addition to the Russian nationalists

feeling little time pressure or heightened war likelihood, the level of disruptive interaction would also be lower. Most Ukrainian moderates agree with President Kuchma's assertion that 'We just have to develop good neighbourly relations with Russia. There are so many economical, historical and spiritual ties binding us together, that any Ukrainian politician who tries to play the anti-Russian card is doomed.'[110]

However, disruptive interaction would not be absent. A moderate Ukrainian leadership, as the Kuchma example has shown, is (within clear limits) more open to policy compromises than a nationalist one. The main questions on which Ukraine cannot compromise concern sovereignty, territorial integrity and freedom to manoeuvre in foreign policy. A moderately led Ukraine will make concessions, but not fall to its knees for Russia. President Kuchma said: 'I did not become president of Ukraine, and I did not walk such a thorny road to become president, just to become a Russian vassal.'[111]

Russian nationalists commonly misinterpret diplomatic initiatives by the former republics as evidence of weakness and a wish for reintegration.[112] When the Russian nationalists see that the accommodating tone of the Ukrainian moderates does not imply any strong wish for integration or union, they could feel cheated by them. It is then possible that Russian nationalists will interpret even the most modest statements and actions as some kind of 'disguised Ukrainian nationalism'. The Russian nationalists could react to this 'disguised nationalism', provoking the Ukrainian moderates. Thus the level of disruptive interaction might rise.

(2) Foreign policy decisions Ukrainian moderates initially brushed aside as over-ideologized nonsense Ukrainian nationalists' fear of Ukraine 'losing a European identity' by closely cooperating with Russia. This view seems, however, slowly to have changed. President Kuchma has also begun to emphasize the Ukrainian return to Europe.[113]

The different 'cognitive filters' of the Russian nationalists and the Ukrainian moderates can lead them to interpret Ukrainian foreign policy initiatives very differently. Ukraine and Russia are, objectively speaking, competitors when it comes to relations with the West. Russia wants the West to recognize it as the heir to the Soviet Union, whereas Ukraine wants the West to treat all fifteen former Soviet republics as equal heirs. There is also competition for Western financial assistance and investment. While the Ukrainian moderates are likely to see their own efforts in this competition as legitimate and normal competition between states, the

Russian nationalists are likely to see such efforts as 'disguised attempts' to unite with the West against Russia. Depending on how fast and to what degree Ukrainian–Western cooperation develops, this might intensify feelings of both time pressure and war likelihood on Russia's part (the latter because of fear that Ukraine might join NATO or another anti-Russian military organization).

(3) Ukrainian territorial integrity Concerning eastern and southern Ukraine, the same considerations apply here as in Scenario one. Also, Ukrainian moderates will try to stop attempts at ESU separatism. This might then give the Russian nationalists a feeling of time pressure and more serious disruptive interaction might evolve.

When the Ukrainian parliament suspended the Crimean constitution and abolished the Crimean presidency on 17 March 1995, the vote was almost unanimous. Likewise, when fourteen days later President Kuchma made the Crimean government responsible to him and not to the Crimean parliament, few domestic opponents spoke up. This suggests that most Ukrainian politicians support a firm stand on the Crimean question. However, all political leaders stress that the Crimean issues will be solved exclusively by peaceful means.

Russian nationalists are likely to consider most actions infringing Crimean autonomy as maltreatment of the Russian population there. The value threat is therefore high. The disruptive interaction is likely to increase, owing to disagreement over what constitutes legitimate action on either side. The Ukrainian authorities will see changes in the autonomous status of Crimea as completely legitimate and no business of Russia's, whereas the Russian nationalists will consider 'attacks' upon Russians in Crimea as an attack upon Russia itself. According to Konstantin Zatulin: 'Whether someone is offended by this or not, politics in the CIS area is Russian domestic politics.'[114] To Ukrainian moderates, therefore, Russia is dangerous not only because it might become an imperialistic power, but because many Russian nationalists do not consider their imperialistic behaviour towards Ukraine to be imperialistic. Since they do not see Ukrainian independence as legitimate, they believe that they do not have to apply the same rules of conduct in their policy towards Ukraine as they do in other interstate relations. As late as June 1995 President Kuchma confirmed that these are not past worries for the Ukrainian leadership. Expressing the concern that radical forces in Moscow might try to play the Ukrainian card, he was asked by *Der Spiegel*'s correspondent what he meant by 'the Ukrainian card.' He answered: 'For example, making territorial demands on Crimea or the coal-rich Donbas.'[115]

There is, however, no reason for the Russian nationalists to perceive a heightened war likelihood as a result of such actions. It is therefore not likely that they would prepare an invasion of Ukraine in response. However, an initially small-scale military action confined to Crimea is not impossible. Crimea is ideally suited for this, since, as one expert on the Russian military, Pavel Baev, has put it: 'For Russia it presents a unique combination of historical sentiments, great-power ambitions, nationalist awareness and military considerations.'[116] Given that, as discussed above, such an initiative might be interpreted differently in Kiev and in Moscow, the potential for escalation might rise. The experience of Chechenia, however, has probably diminished Russia's confidence in the idea of small and successful wars.

(4) The Black Sea Fleet There might be a feeling of time pressure among Russian nationalists who feel that their compatriots in Crimea must be rescued before the Ukrainians are totally in control of the peninsula. This feeling of time pressure is closely linked to the fate of the BSF. If the BSF – and especially its marine infantry troops – is allowed to stay in Crimea, the time pressure will be less, as the Russian nationalists will feel that it is possible to intervene in the defence of the Russian population at any time.

Scenario four: moderates in Ukraine and moderates in Russia

Likelihood of the scenario
The present coexistence of Kuchma and Yeltsin might be considered a moderate–moderate scenario.

Possible spurs for conflict escalation
(1) Russia and Ukrainian independence One can distinguish between Russian moderates who consider an independent Ukraine realistic, and under certain conditions not necessarily bad, and those who, according to Andranik Migranyan, think Ukraine is 'a fragile, artificial, heterogeneous ethno-political entity, without chances of successfully creating its own state'.[117] The latter consider heavy Russian pressure to be unnecessary, and also counterproductive, since it could be used to consolidate the Ukrainian state along anti-Russian lines. It may seem strange to put people who have accepted the idea of an independent Ukraine into the same category as people who cannot imagine that the independence will last, but the reason for calling all of them moderate is that they generally re-

gard a strategy of forcing Ukraine back to Russia as ill-advised.

Corresponding to the two 'moderate' Russian views of Ukrainian independence, there are two views of how Russia should achieve the goals of its Ukraine policy.

Those who see Ukrainian independence as a temporary phenomenon claim that Ukraine, together with the other former Soviet republics, naturally belongs to Russia's sphere of influence. Russia should therefore facilitate but not compel integration. This position was summarized by the Russian deputy minister of defence, Andrei Kokoshin, in an interview in March 1995:

> We have to return to the basic ideas of Russian state formation. I would take as a starting point the middle of the seventeenth century, the period of reunification of Ukraine and Russia. I have always been convinced that by a deep reintegration of our country [here referring not to the Russian Federation, but to the former Soviet Union], we have great chances of success. But I am also convinced that the accomplishment of this reintegration has to be achieved by peaceful means. This is precisely because the citizens of Russia, or Russian citizens, if you will, have suffered the most from the use of force. That is, from uncontrollable expansion, from attempts to save the world, and from their own downfall and destruction.

According to Kokoshin, this destructive urge to save other peoples with the help of the gun is a trait of the Russian national character because the Russians 'lack a healthy feeling of national egoism'.[118]

Those who tend rather to see Ukrainian independence as a lasting fact are correspondingly more vague on the integration issue. A close adviser to President Yeltsin, Dmitry Ryurikov, said in February 1995: 'What degree of integration, and in what areas integration is necessary and beneficial, is a matter for each state to decide for itself. The integration can happen either by bilateral agreements, or within the framework of the CIS. Different interests, different speeds, and different spheres of integration. Nobody will force anybody to anything they do not want to do. There will be no victims.'[119]

So far the 'Ukraine will come back' attitude has prevailed. According to the *Moskovskie novosti* correspondent in Ukraine, Sergei Tikhiy, this has led to the Russian moderates not developing any Ukraine strategy at all, because 'everything is based on the assumption that the younger sister might return any moment'.[120]

Although most Russian moderates, as indeed most Russians in general, probably feel bad about losing Ukraine, they base their Ukraine policy less on emotional arguments than do the nationalists. There are several reasons why Russian moderates still see Ukrainian independence as problematic.

First, Ukraine, like most of the former republics, is considered to be fractured, with a high potential for disintegration and ethnically or socially motivated violent upheaval. Russian defence minister Pavel Grachev said as early as June 1993: 'In our view the most probable scenario is not a direct invasion of Russia but her gradual entanglement in conflicts in neighbouring nations and regions. Given the complex inter-relation and interdependence of the various states and peoples, any armed conflict may evolve into a large-scale war.'[121]

Second, Ukrainian independence represents a loss for Russia because it moves Russia's borders further away from Europe. However, the ever-closer relationship between Russia and Belarus might compensate for the loss of Ukraine in this respect. According to Vladimir Lukin, the chairman of the Russian duma's commission on international politics, there is a view in the Russian political elite that now Russia has been 'removed a thousand kilometres from Europe', this disadvantage will be compensated not through negotiations with unwilling Ukraine, but through the common desire of Russia and Belarus to cooperate.[122]

Third, the difficulties relating to Crimea result from Ukrainian independence. The loss of Crimea is problematic both because of the BSF and the military/strategic importance of Crimea for Russia, and because of the wishes of the predominantly Russian population. No political force in Russia, including the Russian moderates, can be indifferent to these wishes.

(2) Foreign policy decisions As mentioned above, a moderate Ukrainian leadership would not try to cut all ties and totally leave Russia for Europe, seeing a good relationship with Russia as possible, advantageous and historically natural. However, the Ukrainian moderates will also keep a certain distance from Russia. This implies close cooperation only in the economic field, not in military and foreign policy (where cooperation will be essentially bilateral and not conducted through the CIS), and a refusal to accept any supranational organs in the CIS. In February 1995 President Kuchma commented upon CIS cooperation in the following way: 'At the moment we are playing with one set of goalposts. Russia is standing at the penalty spot and scoring goals against everyone.'[123]

Russian moderates, whether they believe that Ukraine can survive or not, feel little time pressure under this scenario. In fact, feelings of time pressure seem to be more present on the Ukrainian side, as illustrated by the process of negotiating the major treaty on friendship and cooperation, initiated in the summer of 1994. The Ukrainian moderates consider it of primary importance to reach agreement with Russia, and get formal acceptance for Ukrainian independence, while Russia is still relatively weak. According to the foreign minister, Udovenko: 'If Ukraine chooses to make no compromises [now] Russia will no longer need to after three or four years.'[124] If Ukraine moves in the direction of NATO membership, however, the feeling of time pressure will grow also on the Russian moderate side. Vladimir Lukin expressed fear of such a development when he asked in *Izvestiya* in May 1995: 'Where will the new borderline be drawn between the pure [Western] and the dirty [Eastern] countries? Will it be between Poland and Ukraine, or between Ukraine and Russia? At Uzhgorod or at Smolensk?'[125]

Ukrainian moderates do not like Russian moderates labelling independent Ukraine as 'a fragile, artificial, heterogeneous ethno-political entity, without chances of successfully creating its own state', and Russian moderates do not like the tendency of even Ukrainian moderates now and then to attach the 'imperialist' label to what they consider perfectly legitimate political initiatives. Disruptive interaction will therefore not disappear under this scenario, but is also unlikely to reach critical levels, and it is likely to decrease with time. According to the Russian chief negotiator with Ukraine, Yuriy Dubinin, this has already started to happen. He commented on the negotiations towards the friendship and cooperation treaty thus: 'The very tone of the talks has changed [after the Kravchuk period]. This change is probably even more important than some accords that have been concluded. Previously we used to throw stones and break pots, but now we are picking up the pieces and endeavoring to stick them together.'[126]

(3) Ukrainian territorial integrity The most likely trigger causing a conflict to escalate into a military dispute under this scenario is the Crimean problem. If the Ukrainian moderates and the Russian moderates were the only parties to the solution of the issue, there would probably not be much time pressure, disruptive interaction or even value threat. The low level of value threat depends on the possibility of a mutually satisfactory solution to the BSF problem. However, a third factor, namely a new pro-Russian Crimean leadership, would be able to limit the room for manoeuvre of

both the Ukrainian and the Russian leadership on the issue.

If Crimean separatism strengthens, a moderate Ukrainian leadership will be under strong domestic pressure to react firmly again, and a moderate Russian leadership will be under strong domestic pressure to support the Russians in Crimea. Initiatives taken on either side are likely to lead to disruptive interaction, and a feeling of time pressure might evolve, since each might try to gain control of the peninsula before the other. The March 1995 actions against the Crimean parliament and president illustrate both the willingness of the moderate Ukrainian and Russian leaderships to accept each other's positions, and the limits to what they can accept. Yeltsin's international aide, Dmitry Ryurikov, told *Izvestiya* on 21 March: 'Events in Crimea are Ukraine's internal affair. However, for well-known reasons the Russian leadership would like the adoption of these decisions to have no result in conflicts that Russia *would have to get involved in settling*' (emphasis added).[127] The document 'Strategic Course of the Russian Federation with Member States of the CIS', presented by Yeltsin in September 1995, states that the guarantee of the rights of Russians 'forms the basis of the country's national security'.[128]

A danger also lies in the potentially different perceptions of the likelihood of war. Whereas the Ukrainian side is likely to interpret a limited Russian military involvement in Crimea as a straightforward attack upon Ukraine, the Russian side might believe in the possibility of confining military operations to Crimea. Here, therefore, a Russian underestimation of the likelihood of war resulting from a limited initiative in Crimea might actually increase the probability of a Russian leadership engaging in such an event.

Chapter 5

Conclusion

This study started by pointing to the significance of Ukraine for European security. Ukraine as an independent state is today an important element in any equation on future security arrangements for Europe. It is furthermore a touchstone for Russian assertiveness in the 'near abroad.' Russian acceptance of Ukrainian independence means better prospects for democratic consolidation in both countries, and makes Russia a more attractive negotiating partner for both the West and east-central Europe. Finally, an unravelling of Ukraine along ethnic lines would mean a serious challenge not only to Ukrainian stability, but to European security itself.

Concerns about undemocratic tendencies in Ukraine, the danger of Russian–Ukrainian tensions escalating into war – possibly with nuclear weapons – and the possibility of an ethnic division of the country along the Dniepr river have been voiced frequently in the West, in east-central Europe, in Russia and not at least in Ukraine itself. My hope is that this study has cast some light on whether or not these anxieties are warranted, and why.

Summary of findings

The evolution of Ukrainian democracy
There are several reasons for optimism about the prospects for continued democratic rule in Ukraine.

A majority both in the population at large and in the political and military elite accept democratic rules of the game. The population shows its acceptance of the new system by a commendably high electoral turnout, despite the fall in living standards that the economic changes have brought with them. The elite has shown its acceptance by peacefully handing over government after electoral defeat, and allowing freedom of expression. The attitudinal markers of democratic consolidation therefore seem to be in place.

Anti-democratic political forces are still marginal, though an increase in their influence can be detected in recent years. Since anti-democratic right-wing extremist groups feed on social degradation, crime and political scandal, UNA-UNSO's progress is an indication of the danger to democracy represented by increasing poverty and crime. There is no reason to believe that Ukrainian society is immune to right-wing extremism, but the marginal position of such extremists suggests that even the current high level of economic deprivation is not enough to cause large parts of Ukrainian society to take up anti-democratic positions of any kind.

The turmoil following the economic and political transformation of the post-communist societies led observers to warn against increasing army involvement in politics. The fear was that this could lead to a replacement of democracies by military dictatorships, as happened in Latin America in the late 1960s. Russia, for example, has experienced increasing military involvement in politics. There are few, if any, signs of this happening in Ukraine today. On the contrary, Ukraine seems to be on the way to establishing civilian control over its military forces. Both the weakness of anti-democratic political forces and the low military involvement in politics suggest that the behavioural markers of democratic consolidation seems to be in place.

Finally, on 28 June 1996 Ukraine peacefully adopted its new constitution. The constitutional marker of democratic consolidation is therefore in place.

It has been a major ambition of both Ukrainian presidents since 1991 to have Ukraine accepted as part of the European community. Ukraine is today willingly adopting Western standards of democracy and human rights, as this is seen as an inherent part of 'becoming European'. The greater attention paid by the West to Ukraine, and Western willingness to recognize Ukraine as a natural and important partner in Europe, are therefore undoubtedly instrumental in encouraging democratic consolidation in Ukraine.

Ethnic mobilization and separatism

The warnings of an ethnic division of Ukraine along the Dniepr seem overstated. In eastern and southern Ukraine, Russians and Russian-speaking Ukrainians are unwilling to mobilize against Ukrainian independence or for separatism, even though a majority in these areas is dissatisfied with independence. A number of factors discourage the Russians of ESU from mobilizing: there is still great confusion of identities in ESU (people have to work out whether they are Russians, Ukrainians or just locals before they can consider mobilizing in the name of one or another ethnicity); Russians and Ukrainian coexist easily, and the ethnic difference between them is blurred by the existence of a large number of Russified Ukrainians; both Russians and Ukrainians are hit equally hard by the economic recession; Russians and Ukrainians enjoy equal career opportunities; the Russians have witnessed the often tragic results of ethnic mobilization in other parts of the former Soviet Union, and the political and economic elite in ESU has developed a strong self-interest in Ukrainian independence. However, redistribution of wealth from ESU to other parts of Ukraine, and a growing gap in living standards between Russians in Ukraine and Russians in Russia, are factors that still could spark demands for reunification with Russia. Western assistance in helping Ukraine not to fall behind Russia in economic reform and economic progress will therefore be a major contribution to ethnic tranquillity in Ukraine.

Ukrainian central authorities have further undermined the potential for ethnic mobilization in ESU by implementing a fairly liberal minority policy. The Russian government has also contributed to stability by not encouraging mobilization against Ukrainian independence.

The situation is somewhat different in Crimea. This is not because the policies of the Ukrainian and the Russian governments here have been essentially different from their policies regarding ESU, but because the support for anti-Ukrainian independence positions is much stronger in Crimea. The aim of the mobilization –separation from Ukraine – is also somewhat less ambitious, and therefore easier to mobilize for, than restoration of the former Soviet Union.

The Ukrainian central authorities smothered the 1994–5 attempts at separating Crimea from Ukraine without violent conflict, but that does not mean that the anti-Ukrainian sentiments in the Crimean population – which got the separatists elected in the first place – have disappeared. The 1994 separatist attempt was impeded by internal disagreement within the separatist leadership, lack of support from Russia and Crimean financial dependence on Kiev. These things could change, and a revival of Crimean separatism therefore cannot be ruled out.

The situation on the peninsula is further complicated by the conflict between the majority Russian population and the Crimean Tatars. The Tatars in Crimea today constitute a socially, economically and politically desperate community in relative isolation from the rest of Crimean society. Their numerical minority *vis-à-vis* the Russians, and their moderate leadership, have so far discouraged them from significant action. However, if they are not included and integrated into Crimea's society and economy, their desperation may burst into violence. A first example of this was the Tatar riots in June 1995.

Political stability has probably been enhanced by the efforts of the OSCE to mediate in the Crimean conflicts – both between Kiev and Simferopol and between the local authorities and the Tatars – while upholding the principle of Ukrainian territorial integrity. None of the parties in the conflicts is totally satisfied with the OSCE role, but that is probably an indication that the OSCE is functioning in its intended role of mediator and stabilizing force. Further assistance in ameliorating relations between Kiev and Simferopol and between Crimean Russians and Crimean Tatars would enhance the prospects for European security.

Russia and Ukraine

The relationship with Russia has been tense ever since Ukraine became independent. The first Ukrainian president, Leonid Kravchuk, did little to improve relations by conducting a foreign policy inspired by western Ukrainian nationalists. While Russia was gradually growing more assertive in its foreign policy from late 1993, Ukraine in 1994 elected a new president advocating closer cooperation with Russia. It soon turned out, however, that though the nationalist rhetoric had gone, Kuchma was just as staunch a defender of Ukrainian interests as Kravchuk had been.

Nevertheless, Ukrainian–Russian relations have improved under Kuchma, though they remain far from normalized. These improvements might be lost, however, if more nationalist politicians came to power in Ukraine or in Russia. I have argued that the advent of a nationalist government in Kiev is largely dependent upon a nationalist government coming to power in Russia, since an anti-Russian electoral success is likely only if the Ukrainian public feels that Ukrainian independence is threatened. Much therefore depends on future developments in Russia.

I have presented three scenarios for the development of the Ukrainian–Russian relationship. The first scenario, a combination of a nationalist government in Ukraine and a nationalist government in Russia, is unlikely but not impossible. This is naturally the scenario containing the highest potential for conflict escalation. With nationalist governments in both countries there is bound to be disruptive interaction. The loss of Ukraine is a major value loss for Russian nationalists. That this should be enough to make Russian nationalists resort to force to bring Ukraine back is still unlikely, given insufficient military capabilities and a weak perception of time pressure or heightened likelihood of war on the Russian side. Also, the serious consequences for domestic stability and the likely damage to Russia's international position that would result from such a conflict are daunting even for Russian hardliners. In any case, most Russian nationalists believe that Ukraine will come back of its own accord.

A military dispute is, however, possible in the longer run if Russian military capabilities increase and the Russian nationalists develop a sufficient feeling of time pressure and heightened likelihood of war. The feeling of time pressure could arise if the Russian nationalists were to get tired of waiting for Ukraine's return and began to worry that the Ukrainian independence experiment might actually succeed and endure. The feeling of heightened war likelihood could be provided by Ukraine joining what Russian nationalists would consider to be an anti-Russian alliance, or by growing separatism in eastern and southern Ukraine or Crimea, combined with harsh Ukrainian actions to thwart this separatism.

The second possible scenario (Scenario three in Chapter 4) envisages a combination of a moderate government in Ukraine and a nationalist government in Russia. The chances of conflict escalation are smaller under this scenario than under the first because the level of disruptive interaction is likely to be lower. Conflict escalation is still possible, however. The level of disruptive interaction might rise if Russian nationalists misinterpreted actions and statements by the Ukrainian moderates as 'disguised Ukrainian nationalism'. If the Russian nationalists do not consider the Ukrainian moderates to be moderates, this scenario could acquire the same conflict potential as the first .

The final scenario – moderate government in both countries – offers the least likelihood of conflict escalation. It is also the scenario that most closely resembles the present situation with Presidents Yeltsin and Kuchma in power. If a military dispute should occur, it would most probably be in response to an 'explosion' in Crimea. That is, ever stronger separatist actions in Crimea would lead both the Ukrainian and the Russian leaderships to feel they must take actions they would rather avoid. Crimea is of high value to both countries; each would expect the other to react, thus creating heightened likelihood of war and time pressure; and the conflict would be accompanied by both verbal and non-verbal disruptive interaction.

Ukraine and the outside world

Ukraine will have to work out its relationship with Russia largely on its own. Though there has been since 1994–5 a remarkable improvement in US–Ukrainian relations, a more modest EU–Ukraine rapprochement, and a search for common ground between the east-central European countries and Ukraine, none of these actors is ready to declare itself on the Ukrainian side in a balancing act against Russia.

However, other countries could do a great deal in laying the groundwork for stable Ukrainian–Russian relations by giving Ukrainian domestic problems more attention. As I have tried to demonstrate, the eruption of domestic Ukrainian conflicts is also the most likely immediate trigger for any Ukrainian–Russian conflict. Political mediation over Crimea, economic support, and promotion of foreign investment serve to strengthen Ukraine at little risk of antagonizing Russia.

Some welcomed the appearance of an independent Ukraine on the European map, some did not. Some still doubt whether Ukraine is capable of independent survival. Few, however, question the importance of Ukrainian independence to European security.

Notes

Chapter 1: Introduction

1 John Edvin Mroz and Oleksandr Pavliuk, 'Ukraine: Europe's Linchpin', *Foreign Affairs*, Vol. 75, No. 3, May/June 1996. Ukraine as 'a strategic pivot in Europe' is a quotation from British Foreign Secretary, Malcolm Rifkind, presented in the same article, p. 59.

2 *Zerkalo Nedely*, No. 14, 6–12 April, 1996.

3 Michael Mandelbaum, 'Preserving the New Peace: The Case Against NATO Expansion', *Foreign Affairs*, Vol. 74, No. 3, May/June 1995, p. 11.

4 See R. J. Rummel, 'Democracies are Less Warlike than Other Regimes', *European Journal of International Relations,* Vol. 1, No. 4, December 1995, pp. 457–9, and Ted R. Gurr and Barbara Harff, *Ethnic Conflict in World Politics,* Westview, Boulder, CO, 1994.

5 See Juan J. Linz and Alfred Stepan, 'Toward Consolidated Democracies', *Journal of Democracy*, Vol. 7, No. 2, April 1996, pp. 14–33.

Chapter 2: The evolution of Ukrainian democracy

1 Artur Bilous, 'Yakoho koloru ideolohiya – chi adaptuyetsya svitovy dosvid na ukrayinskomu hrunti?', *Viche*, No. 6, June 1993, p. 90.

2 Discourse should here be understood as 'a shared vocabulary, figures of speech, standards of argument, criteria of coherence and verification, a certain range of assumptions and problems'. The definition is taken from Joseph Schull, 'What is Ideology? Theoretical Problems and Lessons from Soviet-Type Societies', *Political Studies,* Vol. XL, No. 4, December 1992, p. 731.

3 Victor Nebozhenko, Victor Teren, and Oleksandr Shmorhun, 'Prohrama Kompleksnoyi Sotsialno-Ekonomichnoyi Reformi Ukrayiny', *Rozbudova Derzhavy*, No. 4, April 1993, p. 11.

4 Oleksandr Mayboroda, 'Debyutuye etnopolityka', *Viche*, No. 5, August 1992, p. 133.

5 *Moskovskie novosti,* 6 January 1993.

6 Oleksandr Shmorhun, 'Pro stari zasadi novoho politichnoho myslennya', *Politolohichni Chitannya*, No. 1, 1992, p. 309.

7 *Moskovskie novosti*, 5 September 1993.

8 Larisa Skorik, 'Potreba sinchronnych zusil', *Viche*, No. 9, December 1992, p. 85.

9 *Zerkalo Nedely*, No. 12, 23–29 March 1996.

10 *Zerkalo Nedely*, No. 11, 18–24 March 1995.

11 Author's interview with Victor Musiyaka in Kharkiv, late March 1995.

12 *Zerkalo Nedely*, No. 25, 22–28 June 1996.

13 Oleksiy Mustafin, 'Kolonialnyi syndrom', *UNIAN-Politika,* 7 December 1994 p. 9.

14 *Zamkova Hora,* No. 6, 1994.

15 The UNA programme was presented in *Ukrayinski Obriy*, No. 1, January 1994.

16 *Nezavisimost*, 13 August 1993.

17 *Vseukrayinskie Vedomosti,* 3 November 1994.

18 Interview with Yuriy Tyma in *Kiveskie Vedomosti,* 6 May 1994.

19 *Zerkalo Nedely*, No. 37, 16–22 September 1995.

20 Oleg Pokalchuk, 'UNA-UNSO na puty k vsenarodnoy lyubvi', *UNIAN-Politika*, No. 35, 5–11 September 1995, p. 2.

21 Ibid. p. 2.

22 Maksim But in *Zerkalo Nedely*, No. 25, 24–30 June 1995.

23 Ibid.

24 *Zerkalo Nedely*, No. 18–19, 7–17 May 1996.

25 *The Economist*, 4 February 1995.

26 Vasil Kremen, Yevhen Bazovkin, Myhailo Mishchenko, Victor Nebozhenko, and Petro Sytnyk, 'Sotsialno-politychna sytuatsiya v Ukrayiny: stan i tendentsiyi rozvytku (seredyna 1993 roku), *Politolohichni Chitannya*, No. 1, 1994, p. 43.

27 *Zerkalo Nedely*, 27 July–2 August 1996.

28 *Izvestiya,* 27 July 1995.

29 *Post-Postup*, No. 45, 16–22 December 1994.

30 Interview with General Lopata in *UNIAN-Politika*, No. 21, 23–29 May 1995.

31 Author's interview with General Zhukov, September 1995.

32 Interview with Defence Minister Shmarov in *Vremya*, 29 June 1995, *FBIS-SOV-95-139,* p. 64.

33 *OMRI Daily Digest*, No. 162, 21 August 1995.

34 *Post-Postup*, No. 7, 24 February–1 March 1995.

35 *OMRI Daily Digest*, No. 152, 7 August 1995.

36 Stephen Foye, 'Civilian–Military Tension in Ukraine', *RFE/RL Research Report*, No. 25, Vol. 2, 18 June 1993, p. 63.

37 *Zerkalo Nedely*, No. 28, 13–19 July 1996.

38 Richard Woff, *The Armed Forces of the Former Soviet Union – Evolution, Structure and Personalities,* Portsmouth, Carmichael and Sweet, 1995, Vol. 2, Part 2, Section E, p. 63.

39 Linz and Stepan, 'Toward Consolidated Democracies', p. 15.

40 *The Economist*, 16 April 1994.

41 *Zerkalo Nedely*, No. 26, 29 June–5 July 1996.

42 Linz and Stepan, 'Toward Consolidated Democracies', p. 15.

43 Ibid.

Chapter 3: Ethnic mobilization and separatism

1 Interview with Leonid Kuchma in *Der Spiegel*, No. 27, 1995, pp. 126–30.

2 Throughout the chapter I will use the word Russian to refer to the 22.1 per cent of Ukraine's population who are ethnic Russians according to their passports. However, the reader should bear in mind that whereas this designation applies to only between 40 and 50 per cent of the inhabitants of ESU, more than 75 per cent consider Russian to be their mother tongue (Valeriy Khmelko, 'Tretii rik nezalezhnosti: shcho vyavyly druhi prezydentski vybory', *Ukrayina Segodnya*, No. 6, September 1994, p. 27). There is therefore no doubt that a Russian-speaking majority exists in all eastern and southern Ukraine. The general impression from sociological surveys is also that a majority of the Russian-speaking Ukrainians of ESU have political sympathies close to the Russians of ESU. Political views characteristic of the Russians and Russian-speaking Ukrainians of ESU therefore often constitute majority views in ESU.

3 Rogers Brubaker, 'National Minorities, Nationalising States, and External National Homelands in the New Europe', *Daedalus*, Vol. 124, No. 2, 1995, p. 118.

4 Taras Kuzio and Andrew Wilson, *Ukraine: Perestroika to Independence*, London, Macmillan, 1994, p. 189.

5 *Demokratychna Ukrayina*, 27 April 1995, FBIS-SOV-95-097-S.

6 Aleksandr Tolpygo, 'Resultaty sotsiologicheskikh issledovanii', *Ukrayina Segodnya*, No. 6, 1994, pp. 63–4.

7 *Zerkalo Nedely*, No. 3, 30 March–5 April 1996.

 8 *Moskovskie novosti*, 25 July 1993.

 9 *Post-Postup*, 6–12 October 1994.

10 For a thorough presentation of the historical arguments about the essentially Ukrainian or Russian character of the Donbas, see Andrew Wilson, 'The Donbass between Ukraine and Russia: The Use of History in Political Disputes', *Journal of Contemporary History*, Vol. 30, No. 2, 1995, pp. 265–89.

11 *Moskovskie novosti*, No. 28, 14–21 July 1996.

12 In a spring 1994 sociological survey in eight eastern and southern *oblasts*, the respondents were asked what the first priority of the political authorities should be. Thirty-two per cent said to restore the Soviet Union. Forty-one per cent said 'provide the workers with social guarantees'. It is also interesting to note that fifteen per cent answered 'strengthening of Ukrainian statehood' Aleksandr Tolpygo, 'Resultaty sotsiologicheskikh issledovanii', *Ukrayina Segodnya*, No. 6, September 1994, p. 64.

13 News release from *UNIAN*, FBIS-SOV-95-122.

14 *Zerkalo Nedely*, No. 21, 25–31 May 1996.

15 *Moskovskie novosti,* No. 48, 1990.

16 See Volodymyr Zolotaryov, 'Odesa yak lokomotiv feodalizatsiyi,' *UNIAN-Politika*, 13 September 1994, pp. 18–20.

17 The first three partly correspond to what Charles Tilly has called the three main strands of ethnic mobilization theory – cultural construction theory, structural theory and social-psychological theory. Cultural construction theory focuses on affective macro-level factors such as language, traditions and symbols as causes for ethnic mobilization. Of particular importance here is the crucial role of an intellectual elite in both creating and promoting the ethnic ideology. Structural theory focuses on how political and economic structures affect the political and economic interests of different ethnic groups, and how the articulation of these interests is transferred into ethnic terms. Social-psychological theory stresses psychological needs of each individual, and how similar needs among people create ethnic identity and mobilization at the mass level. See Charles Tilly, 'Ethnic Conflict in the Soviet Union', *Theory and Society*, Vol. 20, No. 5, October 1991, pp. 569–80.

18 This is a modified version of the typology presented in Pål Kolstø, 'The Russian Diaspora: An Identity of its Own', in *The New Russian Diaspora: The Russians outside the Russian Federation in the former USSR: History, Identity and Contemporary Situation,* materials of conference, Latvian Institute of History, Jurmala, 13–15 November, 1992, p. 45.

19 Yaroslav Hrytsak, Oksana Malanchuk and Natalya Chernysh, 'Skhid i

Zakhid: intehratsiya chy dezintehratsiya?', *UNIAN-Politika*, repr. in *Ukraine Today*, RFE/RL Research Institute, 13 September 1994, pp. 12–14.

20 Dmytro Vydrin, 'Naydyem li obshiy yazyk? obyazany!', *Viche*, No. 9, September 1994, p. 69.

21 Dmitry Kornilov, 'Federatsiya – defakto a dezhyure?', *Donetskiy Kryazh*, No. 23, 1993, 26 June–1 July 1993.

22 See for example interview with Stepan Kravchun, representative of the economic elite and director of the giant car manufacturer AvtoZAZ in Zaporizhzhya, *Moskovskie novosti*, No. 47, 9–16 July 1995.

23 John Coakley, 'The Resolution of Ethnic Conflict: Towards a Typology', *International Political Science Review*, Vol. 13, No. 4, October 1992, p. 352.

24 Vojislav Stankovcic, 'Problems and Options in Institutionalizing Ethnic Relations', *International Political Science Review*, Vol. 13, No. 4, October 1992, p. 360.

25 John P. Robinson, Ted. R. Gurr, Erjan Kurbanov, Stephen McHale and Ivan Slepenkov, 'Ethnonationalists and Political Attitudes among Post-Soviet Youth: The Case of Russia and Ukraine', *Political Science and Politics,* September, 1993, pp. 516–21.

26 Vasil Kremen, Yevhen Bazovkin, Myhailo Mishchenko, Victor Nebozhenko and Petro Sytnyk, 'Sotsialno-politychna sytuatsiya v Ukrayiny: stan i tendentsiyi rozvytku (seredyna 1993 roku)', *Politolohichni Chitannya*, No. 1, 1994, p. 50.

27 Taras Kuzio, 'Ukrainian Election Results Point to Growing Regionalism', *Jane's Intelligence Review Pointer*, April 1994, p. 3.

28 *Kievskie Vedomosti*, 21 August 1994.

29 Dmytro Vydrin, 'Naydyem li obshiy yazyk? obyazany', *Viche*, No. 8, August 1994, p. 75.

30 See Aleksandr Vishnyak, 'Byudzhet-95: sotsialnie, regionalnie i politicheskie posledstviya', *UNIAN-Politika*, No. 12, 1995, pp. 7–8, and *Post-Postup*, No. 14, 14–20 April 1995.

31 See interview with Dnipropetrovsk leader and later Ukrainian Prime Minister, Pavlo Lazarenko, *Zerkalo Nedely*, No. 22, 3 June 1995.

32 Andrew Wilson, 'The Growing Challenge to Kiev from Donbass', *RFE/RL Research Report*, Vol. 2, No. 33, Vol. 2, 20 August 1993, p. 8.

33 *The Economist*, 19 June 1993.

34 *Financial Times*, 2 December 1994.

35 *Financial Times,* 15 June 1993.

36 Author's interview with Dmytro Vydrin, Ukrainian presidential administration, 20 March 1995.

37 Author's interview with Volodymyr Ruban, chief editor at UNIAN, UNIAN offices, 22 March 1995.

38 In a June 1994 poll in ESU, only 22 per cent responded in favour of 'a return to the socialist model of development'. Aleksandr Tolpygo, 'Resultaty sotsiologicheskikh issledovanii', *Ukrayina Segodnya*, No. 6, September 1994, p. 64.

39 James Gow, 'Independent Ukraine: The Politics of Security', *International Relations*, Vol. XI, No. 3, December 1992, p. 255.

40 Susan Stewart,'Ukraine's Policy toward its Ethnic Minorities', *RFE/RL Research Report*, Vol. 2, No. 36, 10 September 1993, p. 56.

41 *Radyanska Ukrayina*, 3 November 1989.

42 For details see Susan Stewart, 'Ukraine's Policy toward its Ethnic Minorities', *RFE/RL Research Report*, Vol. 2, No. 36, September 1993, pp. 56–7.

43 Statistics from the Ukrainian Ministry of Nationalities, Migration and Religion, quoted by *INTELNEWS*, 23 June 1995, FBIS-SOV-95-121, p. 68.

44 Roman Szporluk, 'The Strange Politics of Lviv: An Essay in Search of an Explanation', in Zvi Gitelman, ed., *The Politics of Nationality and the Erosion of the USSR*, St Martin's, New York, 1992, p. 219.

45 Arkady Moshes, 'Rossiysko–Ukrainskie otnosheniya v period do 2000 goda', in *Rossiya i ee sosedi* , Moskovskiy Tsentr Karnegi–Carnegie Endowment for International Peace, Moscow, 1995, p. 49.

46 Law on Citizenship, p. 701.

47 See George Schöpflin, 'Nationalism and National Minorities in East and Central Europe', *Journal of International Affairs*, Vol. 45, No. 1, Summer 1991, p. 52.

48 As mentioned, these are Ukrainian nationalistic dissidents from the 1960s, primarily from western Ukraine, many of whom rose to prominent positions in Ukrainian politics during Kravchuk's presidency. Among the best known are Vyacheslav Chornovil, Levko Lukyanenko and Ivan Dzyuba.

49 Vyacheslav Lypynsky (1882–1932), was a Ukrainian historian, philosopher and political activist of Polish origin active in political life in Ukraine from about 1900.

50 Alexander J. Motyl, *Dilemmas of Independence: Ukraine after Totalitarianism*, Council on Foreign Relations Press, New York, 1993, p. 80.

51 Eugene Pyziur, 'Lypyns'kyj's idea of nation', in Jaroslaw Pelenski, ed., *The Political and Social Ideas of Vjaceslav Lypyns'kyj*, special issue of *Harvard Ukrainian Studies* No. 34, December 1985, p. 310.

52 Ibid.

53 See the preamble of the Ukrainian constitution, printed in *Zerkalo Nedely*, No. 28, 13–19 July 1996.

54 Ivan Dzyuba, 'Ukrayina na shlyakhakh derzhavotvorennya', *Viche,* No. 7,
    October 1992, p. 59. See also Les Tanyuk (former leader of the parliamen-
    tary Commission on the Questions of Culture and National Revival), 'Ya i
    My v natsionalnomu postupi', *Viche,* No. 2, February 1993, pp. 116–17,
    and Petro Talanchuk (former Ukrainian Minister of Education) 'Stavka na
    osobistist, vid traditsii Kyevo-Mohilyanskoyi Akademiyi – do
    formuvannya tsilisnoyi natsionalnoyi osvity', *Viche,* No. 1, April, 1992,
    pp. 101–12.

55 Dzyuba, 'Ukrayina na shlyakhakh derzhavotvorennya', p. 58.

56 'Prohrama i statut Narodnoho Rukhu Ukrayiny', Ternopilska oblastna
    drukarnya, Kiev, 1991, p. 16.

57 *Zerkalo Nedely,* No. 23, 8–14 June 1996.

58 *OMRI Daily Digest,* No. 79, part 1, 21 April 1995.

59 Moshes, 'Rossiysko–Ukrainskie otnosheniya', p. 50.

60 Interview with Vyacheslav Irgunov in *Kievskie Vedomosti,* 26 July 1994.

61 Sixty-seven per cent of the Crimean population are Russians, and more
    than 80 per cent use Russian as their first language. Andrew Wilson, 'The
    Growing Challenge to Kiev from Donbass', *RFE/RL Research Report* Vol.
    2, No. 33, 20 August 1993, p. 10.

62 Interview with Leonid Grach in *Vseukrayinskiye Vedomosti,* 17 May 1995,
    FBIS-SOV-95-100.

63 Andrew Wilson, *The Crimean Tatars: A Situation Report on the Crimean
    Tatars for International Alert,* International Alert, London, 1994, p. 32.

64 *Nezavisimaya gazeta,* 5 November 1994.

65 *Moskovskie novosti,* No. 21, 21–29 May 1994.

66 *Nezavisimaya gazeta,* 22 April 1993.

67 *Izvestiya,* 21 March 1995, FBIS-SOV-95-054.

68 See Taras Kuzio, 'The Ukrainian Armed Forces in Crisis', *Jane's Intelli-
    gence Review,* Vol. 7, No. 7, July 1995, p. 306.

69 Valeriy Zaytsev, 'Khronika sobytiy', *Ukrayina Segodnya,* No. 5, 1994,
    p. 107.

70 *Zerkalo Nedely,* No. 15, 1–7 April 1995.

71 See especially *Moskovskie novosti,* No. 29, 23–30 April 1995.

72 Ibid.

73 Valery Zaytsev, 'Krymskiy krizis', *Ukrayina Segodnya,* No. 6, 1994,
    p. 160.

74 Vyacheslav Savchenko, 'Bessilie vlasti kak priznak krymskoy
    gasudarstvennosti', *UNIAN-Politika,* No.14, 4–10 April 1995, p. 9.

75 *Zerkalo Nedely,* No. 22, 3–9 June 1995.

76 Ibid.

77 *Vseukrayinskie Vedomosti*, 6 April 1995.
78 *Moskovskie novosti*, No. 38, 26 May–4 June 1995.
79 *Zerkalo Nedely*, No. 12, 23–29 March 1996.
80 *Zerkalo Nedely*, No. 11, 16–22 March 1996.
81 *Zerkalo Nedely*, No. 13, 30 March–5 April 1996.
82 *Moskovskie novosti*, No. 6, 11–18 February 1996.
83 *Zerkalo Nedely*, No. 17, 27 April–6 May 1996.
84 See the Ukrainian constitution, section 10, paras 134–9. Published in *Zerkalo Nedely*, No. 28, 13–19 July 1996.
85 Ian Bremmer, 'Ethnic Issues in Crimea', *RFE/RL Research Report,* Vol. 2, No. 18, 30 April 1993, p. 25.
86 Kiev INTELNEWS, interview with the head of the Deported Nations Department, Viktor Yakovlev, 1 June 1995, FBIS-SOV-95-106.
87 *Moskovskie novosti*, 31 May 1992.
88 Andrew Wilson, *The Crimean Tatars*, p. 6.
89 *Nezavisimaya gazeta*, 2 February 1993.
90 Milli Firka was the name of a political party created by radical leaders of the Tatar intelligentsia in June 1917, to fight for Tatar political autonomy. Alan W. Fisher, *The Crimean Tatars*, Hoover Institution Press, Stanford, 1987.
91 Wilson, *The Crimean Tatars.* p. 7.
92 *Zerkalo Nedely*, No, 22, 3–9 June 1995.
93 *Moskovskie novosti*, No. 3, 21–28 January 1996.
94 *Financial Times*, 19 July 1995.
95 *Literaturnaya gazeta*, 5 July 1995, FBIS-SOV-95-140-S, p. 68.
96 These are the town councils of Alushta, Yalta, Feodosia, Kerch, Sudak and Dzhankoy: *Nezavisimaya gazeta*, 27 March 1993.
97 *Nezavisimaya gazeta*, 3 October 1992.
98 Andrew Wilson, *The Crimean Tatars*, p. 22.
99 *Zerkalo Nedely*, No. 22, 3–9 June 1995.

Chapter 4: Ukraine and Russia

1 Quoted in Rem Symonenko, 'Doktrynu Monro-Mihranyana proholosheno, shcho dali?', *Polityka i Chas*, No. 6, June 1994, p. 17.
2 Klara Gudzik, 'Mizh rosiyskoyu hehemoniyeyo ta bayduzhistyu Zakhodu,' *UNIAN-Politika,* 29 August 1994, p. 15.
3 *Jamestown Broadcast Monitor*, 6 October 1995.
4 An analysis paper prepared by the Institute of Europe at the Russian Academy of Sciences in 1995, under the leadership of the influential

Russian analyst, Sergei Karaganov, strongly warns against making the CIS the vehicle for integration. See Karaganov and others, *Geopoliticheskie Peremeny v Yevrope, Politika Zapada i Alternativy dlya Russii*, Reports of the Institute of Europe No. 19, Moscow, 1995.

5　See Andrei Zagorski, 'What Kind of the CIS Would Do?', *Aussenpolitik*, Vol. 46, No. 3, 1995.

6　'Osnovni napryamy zovnishnoyi polityky Ukrayiny', *Uryadovii kuryer*, No. 111, 24 July 1993.

7　See statement by the Ukrainian Deputy Minister of Defence, Ivan Bizhan, *Haryacha Liniya* [Independent press centre], 12 September 1994.

8　*Moskovskie novosti*, No. 6, 1–18 April 1996.

9　*Zerkalo Nedely*, No. 15, 13–19 April 1996.

10　Interview with Kravchuk, *Suchasnist,* No. 1, January 1992, p. 18.

11　See Volodymyr Horbulin, 'Nasha meta, Nasha dolya – Mistse Ukrayiny v suchasniy Yevropy', *Polityka i Chas*, No. 1, January 1996, pp. 3–8.

12　*Zerkalo Nedely*, No. 23, 8–14 June 1996.

13　*Zerkalo Nedely*, No. 26, 29 June–1 July 1996.

14　*Moskovskie novosti*, No. 19, 12–19 May 1996.

15　For details see Sergei Tikhii, 'Chernoe zoloto iz-za morya Chornovo', *Moskovskie novosti*, No. 9, 5–12 February 1995.

16　*Moskovskie novosti*, No. 14, 7–14 April 1996.

17　*Ukraino–Rossiyskoye kommyunike* [Ukrainian–Russian Communiqué], para. 11, published in *Zerkalo Nedely*, No. 23, 10–16 June 1995.

18　*Zerkalo Nedely*, No. 26, 29 June–5 July 1996.

19　*Jamestown Broadcast Monitor,* 10 October 1995.

20　*Jamestown Broadcast Monitor*, 31 October 1995.

21　Arkady Moshes, 'Rossiysko–Ukrainskie otnosheniya v period do 2000 goda', in *Rossiya i ee sosedi,* Moskovski Tsentr Karnegi–Carnegie Endowment for International Peace, Moscow, 1995, p. 32.

22　*Financial Times,* 7 May 1993.

23　Dmytro Vydrin, 'Ukraine on the Nuclear See-saw,' *Political Thought,* No. 2, 1994, p. 197.

24　Ibid.

25　William H. Kincade, 'Nuclear Weapons in Ukraine: Hollow Threat, Wasting Asset,' *Arms Control Today*, Vol. 23, No. 6, July/August, 1993, p. 15.

26　*The Economist*, 14 August 1993.

27　A. Tolpygo, 'Resultaty sotsiologicheskikh issledovanii', *Ukrayina Segodnya*, No. 5, May 1994, p. 69.

28　*Nezavisimaya gazeta*, 22 April 1993.

29 *Vseukrayinskie Vedomosti,* 14 September 1994.

30 Dmytro Vydrin, 'Naydyem li obschyi yazyk ? obyazany!', *Viche*, No. 9, September 1994, p. 70.

31 Interview with Hennadiy Udovenko in *Nezavisimost*, 7 September 1994.

32 *Financial Times*, 7 May 1993.

33 Strobe Talbott, 'The United States and Ukraine: Broadening the Relationship', *US Department of State Dispatch,* Vol. 4, No. 27, 5 July 1993, p. 480.

34 See Michael Cox, *US Foreign Policy after the Cold War: Superpower Without a Mission?,* Chatham House Papers, Royal Institute of International Affairs/Pinter, London, 1995, pp. 54–69.

35 Eugene B. Rumer, 'Eurasia Letter: Will Ukraine Return to Russia?', *Foreign Policy*, No. 96, Fall 1994, p. 143.

36 *Zerkalo Nedely*, No.17, 24 April–6 May, 1996.

37 Zbigniew Brzezinski, 'A Plan for Europe', *Foreign Affairs*, Vol. 74, No. 1, January/February 1995, p. 38.

38 Vladimir P. Lukin, 'Our Security Predicament', *Foreign Policy*, No. 88, Fall 1992, p. 63.

39 Quoted in Taras Kuzio, 'Yakir stabilnosti dlya kontinentu – stratehichna vazhlivist Ukrayiny dlya bezpaky Zakhodu, *Polityka i Chas*, No. 4, April 1996, p. 26.

40 Anders Åslund, 'Ukraine's Turnaround,' *Foreign Policy*, Vol. 25, No. 100, Fall 1995, p. 139.

41 *The Times*, 4 April 1996.

42 The Hungarians live in a fairly compact area in the Berehove and Vynohradiv *rayons*, which border on Hungary.

43 The Treaties of Saint-Germain (1919) and Trianon (1920) gave the Zakarpattya region to Czechoslovakia, which ruled the region until 1938.

44 Ilya Prizel, 'The Influence of Ethnicity on Foreign Policy – The Case of Ukraine', in R. Szporluk, ed., *National Identity and Ethnicity in Russia and the New States of Eurasia*, M.E. Sharpe, London, 1994, p. 112.

45 Tamara Kutsay, 'Podorozh sotsialista v kapitalistichne maybutnye', *UNIAN-Politika*, 7 December 1994, p. 3.

46 Ilya Prizel, 'The Influence of Ethnicity', p. 112.

47 Ian Brzezinski, 'Polish-Ukrainian Relations: Europe's Neglected Strategic Axis', *Survival,* Vol. 35, No. 3, Autumn 1993, p. 26.

48 Piotr Kolodziejczyk, 'Poland: A Future NATO Ally', *NATO Review*, October 1994, Vol. 42, No. 5, p. 8.

49 Marek Janusz Calka, 'Relations with Ukraine', in *The Yearbook of Polish Foreign Policy*, PISM, Warsaw, 1995, p. 1.

50 Oleh Dorozhovets, 'Chy zarazyv Hennadiy Udovenko svoye vidomstvo alerhiyeyu na Varshavu', *UNIAN-Politika,* 7 December 1994, p. 7.

51 See Bohdan Osadchuk, 'Varshava pobyvayetsya, chy ne zminyt Kyyiv zovnishnoyi polityky', *UNIAN-Politika,* 8 August 1994, p. 4.

52 Jan B. de Weydenthal, 'Poland's Eastern Policy', *RFE/RL Research Report*, Vol. 3, No. 7, 18 February, 1994, p. 13.

53 *Zerkalo Nedely*, No. 23, 8–14 June 1996.

54 By the southernmost part of Odessa *oblast* is meant the counties of Reni, Bolhrad, Izmayil, Kiliya, Tarutine, Artsiz, Tatarbunari, Sarata, and Bilhorod-Dnistrovsky. See B. Boechko, 'Severnaya Bukovyna i Pridunavye–iskonnaya territoriya Ukrainy', *Polityka i Vremya*, No. 5, May 1992, pp. 47–51 and No. 6, June 1992, pp. 66–71.

55 *Jamestown Broadcast Monitor*, 2 November 1995.

56 *Zerkalo Nedely*, No. 49, 9–15 December 1995.

57 Michael Shafir and Dan Ionescu, 'The Tangled Path Toward Democracy', *Transition*, Vol. 1, 30 January 1995, p. 54.

58 B. Boechko, 'Severnaya Bukovyna i Pridunavye'.

59 *Dnyestrovskaya Pravda*, 12 March 1993.

60 Taras Kuzio, 'Ukraine and its Near Abroad', *Politychna Dumka,* No. 3, 1994, p. 203.

61 Katerina Kindras, 'Nad Prydnistrovyam znovu zakhmarene nebo', *UNIAN-Politika*, 19 August 1994, p. 3.

62 See Dan Ionescu, 'Little Hope for Russian Withdrawal from Moldova', *Jane's Intelligence Review*, Vol. 8, No. 7, July 1996, p. 293.

63 Karoly Kiss and Volodimir R. Sidenko, 'Ukraine on the Way toward Economic Stabilization and Independence', *Eastern European Economics*, Vol. 31, No. 2, Winter 1992–3, p. 77.

64 *The Economist*, 13 February 1993.

65 Interview with Oleksandr S. Samodurov, responsible for the relations with Russia in the Ukrainian ministry of foreign economic relations and trade, printed in *Polityka i Chas*, No. 2, February 1996.

66 Matthew J. Sagers, 'The Energy Industries of the Former USSR; a Mid-year Survey', *Post-Soviet Geography*, Vol. 34, No. 6, June 1993, p. 389.

67 *Moskovskie novosti*, No. 19, 19–26 March 1994.

68 David R. Marples, 'Ukraine, Belarus, and the Energy Dilemma,' *RFE/RL Research Report* No. 27, Vol. 2, 2 July 1993, p. 40.

69 See Ustina Markus, 'Energy Crisis Spurs Ukraine and Belarus to Seek Help Abroad', *Transition*, Vol. 2, No. 9, 3 May 1996, p. 16.

70 Karaganov et al., *Geopoliticheskie peremeny v Yevrope*. p. 29.

71 Dmytro Vydrin, 'Naydyem li obschyi yazyk? obyazany!', p. 62.

72 Author's interview with Dmytro Vydrin at the presidential administration building in Kiev, 20 March 1995.

73 'A nam shcho robyty z Rosiyeyu?', roundtable discussion on Ukrainian–Russian relations published in *Polityka i Chas*, No. 3, March 1996, p. 17.

74 Other elements of Ukrainian exports to Russia are: metallurgical goods and ore concentrates 32 per cent, machine building 26 per cent and chemical products 7 per cent. Interview with Oleksandr S. Samodurov, published in *Polityka i Chas*, No. 2, February 1996.

75 Interview with Samodurov, *Polityka i Chas*, No. 2, p. 41.

76 Sherman W. Garnett, 'The Integrationist Temptation', *The Washington Quarterly,* Vol. 18, No. 2. Spring 1995, p. 40.

77 Brigitte Sauerwein, 'Rich in Arms, Poor in Tradition', *International Defense Review*, Vol. 26, No. 4, April 1993, p. 317.

78 For details see Oleg Bodruk, 'The Armed Forces of Ukraine', paper presented at the conference 'Security Dilemmas in the CIS Region', Royal Institute of International Affairs, Chatham House, London, 28–29 September, 1995, pp. 1–2.

79 Richard Woff, *The Armed Forces of the Former Soviet Union,* Carmichael and Sweet, Portsmouth, 1995, Vol. 2, Part 2, Section E, p. 23.

80 See, 'Restructuring the Ukrainian Ground Forces', *Jane's Intelligence Review Pointer,* July 1994, p. 3, and Stepan Oliynik, 'Poki shcho naybilshe bahatstvo Ukrayiny – tse yiyi armiya', *UNIAN-Politika,* 12 July 1994, p. 17.

81 Sergey Zgurets, 'Ukrayina dognala i peregnala vsekh, no s ney, pokhozhe, nikto ne sorevnovalsya', *UNIAN-Politika*, No. 44, 31 October–9 November, 1995, p. 3.

82 Ibid.

83 Stepan Oliynik, 'Poki shcho naiybilshe bahatstvo Ukrayini – tse yiyi armiya', p. 17.

84 Richard Woff, *The Armed Forces of the Former Soviet Union,* p. 29.

85 Charles J. Dick, 'The Military Doctrine of Ukraine', *The Journal of Slavic Military Studies*, Vol. 7, No. 3, 1994, p. 516.

86 Stephen Foye, 'Civilian–Military Tension in Ukraine', *RFE/RL Research Report* Vol. 2, No. 25, 18 June 1993, p. 63.

87 Ibid.

88 *Zerkalo Nedely*, No. 24, 15–21 June 1996.

89 *Vechirniy Kyiv*, 24 September 1994.

90 *Zerkalo Nedely*, No. 24, 15–21 June 1996.

91 Oliynik, 'Poki shcho naiybilshe bahatstvo Ukrayini – tse yiyi armiya', p. 16.

92 Interview with Boris Tarasyuk in *Transition*, Vol. 1, No. 13, 28 July 1995, p. 20.

93 See Scott Parrish, 'Chaos in Foreign Policy Decision-Making', *Transition*, Vol. 2, No. 10, 17 May 1996, pp. 30–33.

94 *Zerkalo Nedely*, No. 51, 23–29 December 1995.

95 *Zerkalo Nedely*, No. 6, 20–26 April 1996.

96 Michael Brecher, *Crises in World Politics,* Pergamon, Oxford, 1993, p. 142.

97 Igor Kliamkin, 'Russian Statehood, the CIS, and the Problem of Security', in *The Emergence of Russian Foreign Policy*, United States Institute of Peace Press, Washington, DC, 1994, pp. 111–12.

98 *Izvestiya*, 12 October 1995.

99 Stepan Romanchuk, 'Tretya sessiya parlamenta: novoye bolshinstvo i Porosuminnya', *UNIAN-Politika*, No. 2, January 1995, p. 1.

100 Gudzik, 'Mizh rosiyskoyu hehemoniyeyu ta bayduzhistyu Zakhodu', p. 16.

101 *Kievskie Vedomosti*, 29 March 1995.

102 Yurii Kostenko, 'Natsionalna bezpeka – zasib zberezhennya ukrayinskoho narodu', *Rozbudova Derzhavy*, No. 1, June 1992, p. 22.

103 Dmytro Pavlychko, 'Yevropa vidchula shcho vona bilsha nizh zdavalos,' *Viche*, No. 8, November 1992, p. 141.

104 Gudzik, 'Mizh rosiyskoyu hehemoniyeyo ta bayduzhistyu Zakhodu', p. 16.

105 Jeremy Lester, 'Russian Political Attitudes to Ukrainian Independence', *Journal of Communist Studies and Transition Politics*, Vol. 10, No. 2, June 1994, p. 217.

106 Quoted in Sven Gunnar Simonsen, *Politics and Personalities – Key Actors in the Russian Opposition*, PRIO Report, Oslo, No. 2, 1996, p. 119.

107 Ola Tunander, 'New European Dividing Lines?', in *Norway Facing a Changing Europe,* conference proceedings, Norwegian Foreign Policy Studies, No. 79, 1992, p. 55.

108 *Zerkalo Nedely,* No. 32, 12–19 August 1995.

109 See Lyubov Abessonova, 'Armiya i vybory', *Ukrayina Segodnya,* No. 5, 1994, pp. 42–6, and Oleksandr Shtyka, 'Armiya v politychyni systemi ukrayinskoho suspilstva', *Politolohichni Chytannya,* No. 2, 1994, pp. 67–83.

110 *Zerkalo Nedely*, No. 41, 14–20 October 1995.

111 *Nezavisimaya gazeta,* 28 October 1994.

112 See Garnett, 'The Integrationist Temptation', p. 38.

113 Interview with President Kuchma in *Der Spiegel*, No. 27, 1995.

114 Rem Symonenko, 'Doktrynu Monro-Mihranyana proholosheno, shcho dali?', *Polityka i Chas*, No. 6, June 1994, p. 16.
115 Interview with Leonid Kuchma in *Der Spiegel*, No. 27, 1995, pp. 126–30.
116 Pavel K. Baev, 'Russian Military Thinking and the Near Abroad', *Jane's Intelligence Review*, Vol. 6, No. 12, December 1994, p. 533.
117 *Nezavisimaya gazeta*, 18 January 1994.
118 Interview with Andrei Kokoshin in *Moskovskie novosti*, No. 15, 26 February–5 March 1995.
119 *Moskovskie novosti*, No. 13, 19–26 February 1995.
120 *Moskovskie novosti*, 19–26 March 1995.
121 Quoted in Leon Aron, 'The Emergent Priorities of Russian Foreign Policy', in Leon Aron and Kenneth M. Jensen, eds, *The Emergence of Russian Foreign Policy*, United States Institute of Peace Press, Washington, DC, 1994, p. 24.
122 Interview with Vladimir Lukin in *Zerkalo Nedely*, No. 11, 18–24 March 1995.
123 *Financial Times*, 10 February 1995.
124 ITAR-TASS, 30 November, 1994, translated in FBIS-SOV-94-231.
125 *Izvestiya*, 12 May 1995.
126 Interview with Yuriy Dubinin in *Rabochaya Tribuna*, 11 March 1995, English version in FBIS-SOV-95-049, pp. 12–13.
127 *Izvestiya*, 21 March 1995, English version in FBIS-SOV-95-054.
128 Kathleen Mihalisko, 'Yeltsin Outlines Strategy for a Renewed Superpower', *Jamestown Prism,* March 1995.

Bibliography

Abessonova, Lyubov (1994), 'Armiya i vybory', *Ukrayina Segodnya,* No. 5, pp. 42–6.

Armstrong, John A. (1990), *Ukrainian Nationalism*, 3rd edn, Ukrainian Academic Press, Englewood, Colorado.

Aron, Leon, (1994), 'The Emergent Priorities of Russian Foreign Policy', in Leon Aron and Kenneth M. Jensen, eds, *The Emergence of Russian Foreign Policy*, United States Institute of Peace Press, Washington, pp. 17–34.

Åslund, Anders (1995), 'Ukraine's Turnaround', *Foreign Policy*, Vol. 25, No. 100, Fall, pp. 125–43.

Baev, Pavel K. (1994), 'Russian Military Thinking and the "Near Abroad"', *Jane's Intelligence Review,* Vol. 6, No. 12, December, pp. 531–3.

Bilous, Artur (1993), 'Yakoho koloru ideolohiya – chi adaptuyetsya svitovy dosvid na ukrayinskomu hrunti?', *Viche*, No. 6, June, pp. 80–90.

Bodruk, Oleg (1995), 'The Armed Forces of Ukraine', paper presented at the conference 'Security Dilemmas in the CIS Region', Royal Institute of International Affairs, Chatham House, London, 28–29 September. Revised version in Roy Allison and Christoph Bluth (eds), *Security Dilemmas in Russia and Eurasia*, RIIA, London, forthcoming 1997.

Boechko, B. (1992), 'Severnaya Bukovyna i Pridunavye – iskonnaya territoriya Ukrainy', *Polityka i Vremya*, No. 5, May, pp. 47–51 and No. 6, June, pp. 66–71.

Brecher, Michael (1993), *Crises in World Politics: Theory and Reality*, Pergamon, Oxford.

Bremmer, Ian (1993), 'Ethnic Issues in Crimea', *RFE/RL Research Report*, Vol. 2, No. 18, 30 April, pp. 24–28.

Brubaker, Rogers (1995), 'National Minorities, Nationalising States, and External National Homelands in the New Europe', *Daedalus*, Vol. 124, No. 2, pp. 107–32.

Brzezinski, Ian (1993), 'Polish–Ukrainian Relations: Europe's Neglected Strategic Axis', *Survival*, Vol. 35, No. 3, Autumn, pp. 26–37.

Brzezinski, Zbigniew (1995), 'A Plan for Europe', *Foreign Affairs*, Vol. 74, No. 1, January/February, pp. 26–42.

Calka, Marek Janusz (1995), 'Relations with Ukraine', in *The Yearbook of Polish Foreign Policy*, Department of Studies and Planning – PISM, at the Polish Ministry of Foreign Affairs, Warsaw, p. 17.

Coakley, John (1992), 'The Resolution of Ethnic Conflict: Towards a Typology', *International Political Science Review*, Vol. 13, No. 4, pp. 343–58.

Cox, Michael (1995), *US Foreign Policy after the Cold War: Superpower Without a Mission?*, Royal Institute of International Affairs/Pinter, London.

Dashkevich, Yaroslav (1992), 'Ukrayintsi v Krimu (XV - pochatok XX stolittya)', *Suchasnist*, No. 4, April, pp. 96–104.

Dick, Charles J. (1994), 'The Military Doctrine of Ukraine', *Journal of Slavic Military Studies*, Vol. 7, No. 3, 1994, pp. 507–20.

Dorozhovets, Oleh (1994), 'Chy zarazyv Hennadiy Udovenko svoye vidomstvo alerhiyeyu na Varshavu', *UNIAN-Politika*, repr. in *Ukraine Today*, RFE/RL Research Institute, 7 December, pp. 7–8.

Dzyuba, Ivan (1992), 'Ukrayina na shlyakhakh derzhavotvorennya', *Viche*, No. 7, October, pp. 49–60.

Fisher, Alan W. (1987), *The Crimean Tatars*, Studies of Nationalities in the USSR, Hoover Institution Press, Stanford.

Foye, Stephen (1993), 'Civilian–Military Tension in Ukraine', *RFE/RL Research Report*, Vol. 2, No. 25, 18 June pp. 60–66.

Garnett, Sherman W. (1995), 'The Integrationist Temptation', *Washington Quarterly*, Vol. 18, No. 2, Spring, pp. 35–44.

Gow, James (1992), 'Independent Ukraine: The Politics of Security', *International Relations*, Vol. XI, No. 3, December, pp. 253–67.

Gudzik, Klara (1994), 'Mizh rosiyskoyu hehemoniyeyo ta bayduzhistyu Zakhodu', *UNIAN-Politika*, repr. in *Ukraine Today* RFE/RL Research Institute, 29 August, pp. 15–17.

Gurr, Ted R., and Harff, Barbara (1994), *Ethnic Conflict in World Politics*, Westview, Boulder, CO.

Halenko, Oleksandr (1993), 'Posylayu varti druzhby blahopobazhannya', *Viche*, No. 5, May, pp. 146–52.

Haran, Oleksiy (1994), 'Istoria Rukhu: kontseptualni ta ideolohichni problemy', *Suchasnist*, No. 11, pp. 97–101.

Horbulin, Volodymyr (1996), 'Nasha meta, Nasha dolya - Mistse Ukrayiny v suchasniy Yevropy', *Polityka i Chas*, No. 1, January, p. 3–8.

Hrytsak, Yaroslav, Malanchuk, Oksana, and Chernysh, Natalya (1994), 'Skhid

Bibliography

i Zakhid: intehratsiya chy dezintehratsiya', *UNIAN-Politika*, repr. in *Ukraine Today*, RFE/RL Research Institute, 13 September, pp. 12–14.

Hurzhiy, Oleksandr (1992), 'Susalna pozolota chi istorichna bezvykhid ?', *Viche*, No. 3, June, pp. 101–9.

Ionescu, Dan (1996), 'Little Hope for Russian Withdrawal from Moldova', *Jane's Intelligence Review*,Vol. 8, No. 7, July, pp. 292–3.

Karaganov, S. et al. (1995), *Geopoliticheskie Peremeny v Yevrope, Politika Zapada i Alternativy dlya Russii*, Reports of the Institute of Europe, No. 19, Moscow.

Khmelko, Valeriy (1994), 'Tretiy rik nezalezhnosti: shcho vyavyly druhi prezydentski vybory', *Ukrayina Segodnya*, No. 6, September, pp. 22–30.

Kincade, William H. (1993), 'Nuclear Weapons in Ukraine: Hollow Threat, Wasting Asset', *Arms Control Today*, Vol. 23, No. 6, July/August, pp. 13–18.

Kindras, Katerina (1994), 'Nad Prydnistrovyam znovu zakhmarene nebo', *UNIAN-Politika*, repr. in *Ukraine Today*, RFE/RL Research Institute, 19 August, p. 3.

Kiss, Karoly and Sidenko, Volodimir R. (1992/3), 'Ukraine on the Way toward Economic Stabilization and Independence', *Eastern European Economics*, Winter, Vol. 31, No. 6, pp. 65–93.

Kliamkin, Igor (1994), 'Russian Statehood, the CIS, and the Problem of Security', in *The Emergence of Russian Foreign Policy*, United States Institute of Peace Press, Washington, DC, pp. 107–118.

Kolodziejczyk, Piotr (1994), 'Poland: A Future NATO Ally', *NATO Review*, Vol. 42, No. 5, October, pp. 7–10.

Kolstø, Pål (1992), 'The Russian Diaspora: An Identity of its Own', in *The New Russian Diaspora: The Russians Outside the Russian Federation in the Former USSR: History, Identity and Contemporary Situation*, materials of conference, Latvian Institute of History, Jurmala, 13–15 November, pp. 38–66.

Kornilov, Dmitry (1993), 'Federatsiya – defakto a dezhyure?', *Donetskiy Kryazh*, No. 23, 26 June–1 July.

Kostenko, Yurii (1992), 'Natsionalna bezpeka – zasib zberezhennya ukrayinskoho narodu', *Rozbudova Derzhavy*, No. 1, June, pp. 20–23.

Kremen, Vasil, Bazovkin, Yevhen, Mishchenko, Myhailo, Nebozhenko, Victor, and Sytnyk, Petro (1994), 'Sotsialno-politychna sytuatsiya v Ukrayiny: stan i tendentsiyi rozvytku (seredyna 1993 roku)', *Politolohichni Chitannya*, No. 1, pp. 22–73.

Kulyk, Volodymyr (1992), ' Povtorennya pereydenoho. Ukrayinska revolyutsia: 1917–1991', *Suchasnist*, No. 2, February, pp. 59–72.

Kutsay, Tamara (1994), 'Podorozh sotsialista v kapitalistichne maybutnye', *UNIAN-Politika,* repr. in *Ukraine Today,* RFE/RL Research Institute, 7 December, pp. 3–5.

Kuzio, Taras (1994), 'Ukraine and its "Near Abroad"', *Politychna Dumka,* No. 3, pp. 198–207.

Kuzio, Taras (1994), 'Ukrainian Election Results Point to Growing Regionalism', *Jane's Intelligence Review Pointer,* April, p. 3.

Kuzio, Taras (1995), 'The Ukrainian Armed Forces in Crisis', *Jane's Intelligence Review,* Vol. 7, No. 7, pp. 305–6.

Kuzio, Taras (1995), 'Ukraine and the Expansion of NATO', *Jane's Intelligence Review,* Vol. 7, No. 9, pp. 389–91.

Kuzio, Taras (1996), 'Yakir stabilnosti dlya kontinentu – stratehichna vazhlivist Ukrayiny dlya bezpeky Zakhodu', *Polityka i Chas,* No. 4, April, pp. 26–9.

Kuzio, Taras, and Wilson, Andrew (1994), *Ukraine: Perestroika to Independence,* London, Macmillan.

Lester, Jeremy (1994), 'Russian Political Attitudes to Ukrainian Independence', *Journal of Communist Studies and Transition Politics,* Vol. 10, No. 2, June, pp. 193–232.

Linz, Juan J., and Stepan, Alfred (1996), 'Toward Consolidated Democracies', *Journal of Democracy,* Vol. 7, No. 2, April, pp. 14–33.

Lukin, Vladimir P. (1992), 'Our Security Predicament', *Foreign Policy,* No. 88, Fall, pp. 57–75.

Mandelbaum, Michael (1995), 'Preserving the New Peace: The Case Against NATO Expansion', *Foreign Affairs,* Vol. 74, No. 3, May/June, pp. 9–13.

Markus, Ustina (1996), 'Energy Crisis Spurs Ukraine and Belarus to Seek Help Abroad', *Transition,* 3 May, pp. 14–18.

Marples, David R. (1993), 'Ukraine, Belarus, and the Energy Dilemma', *RFE/RL Research Report,* Vol. 2, No. 27, 2 July, pp. 39–44.

Mayboroda, Oleksandr (1992), 'Debyutuye etnopolityka', *Viche,* No. 5, August, pp. 122–34.

Moshes, Arkady (1994), 'Povernetsya li rossiyskiy orel k ukrainskomu trezubtsu', *Novoye Vremya,* No. 27, pp. 10–12.

Moshes, Arkady (1995), 'Rossiysko–Ukrayinskie otnosheniya v period do 2000 goda', in *Rossiya i ee sosedi,* Moskovski Tsentr Karnegi–Carnegie Endowment for International Peace, Moscow, pp. 26–53.

Motyl, Alexander J. (1993), *Dilemmas of Independence: Ukraine after Totalitarianism,* Council on Foreign Relations Press, New York.

Mroz, John Edvin, and Pavliuk, Oleksandr (1996), 'Ukraine: Europe's Linchpin', *Foreign Affairs,* Vol. 75, No. 3, May/June, pp. 52–62.

Bibliography

Mustafin, Oleksiy (1994), 'Kolonialnyi syndrom', *UNIAN-Politika*, repr. in *Ukraine Today*, RFE/RL Research Institute, 7 December, pp. 9–11.

Nebozhenko, Victor, Teren, Victor, and Shmorhun, Oleksandr (1993), 'Prohrama Kompleksnoyi Sotsialno-Ekonomichnoyi Reformi Ukrayiny', *Rozbudova Derzhavy*, No. 4, April, pp. 4–63.

Oliynik, Stepan (1994), 'Poki shcho naiybilshe bahatstvo Ukrayiny – tse yiyi armiya', *UNIAN-Politika*, repr. in *Ukraine Today*, RFE/RL Research Institute, 12 July, pp. 16–17.

Osadchuk, Bohdan (1994), 'Varshava pobyvayetsya, chy ne zminyt Kyyiv zovnishnoyi polityky', *UNIAN-Politika*, repr. in *Ukraine Today*, RFE/RL Research Institute, 8 August, pp. 4–5.

'Osnovni napryamy zovnishnoyi polityky Ukrayiny', *Uryadovii kuryer*, No. 111, 24 July 1993.

Parrish, Scott (1996), 'Chaos in Foreign Policy Decision-Making', *Transition*, Vol. 2, No. 10, 17 May, pp. 30–33.

Pavlychko, Dmytro (1992), 'Yevropa vidchula shcho vona bilsha nizh zdavalos', *Viche*, No. 8, November, pp. 139–143.

Pokalchuk, Oleg (1995), 'UNA-UNSO na puty k vsenarodnoy lyubvi', *UNIAN-Politika*, No. 35, 5–11 September, pp. 2–3.

Polonska Vasylenko, Nataliya (1993), *Istoriya Ukraiyiny, u dvokh tomakh*, Lybid, Kiev.

Prizel, Ilya (1994), 'The Influence of Ethnicity on Foreign Policy: The Case of Ukraine', in R. Szporluk, ed., *National Identity and Ethnicity in Russia and the New States of Eurasia*, M. E. Sharpe, London, pp. 103–28.

Pyziur, Eugene (1985), 'Lypyns'kyj's idea of nation', in Pelenski, ed., *The Political and Social Ideas of Vjaceslav Lypyns'kyj*, special issue of *Harvard Ukrainian Studies*, No. 3–4, December, pp. 302–25.

Robinson, John. P., Gurr, Ted. R., Kurbanov, Erjan, McHale, Stephen, and Slepenkov, Ivan (1993), 'Ethnonationalist and Political Attitudes among Post-Soviet Youth: The Case of Russia and Ukraine', *Political Science and Politics*, September, pp. 516–21.

Romanchuk, Stepan (1995), 'Tretya sessiya parlamenta: novoye bolshinstvo i Porosuminnya', *UNIAN-Politika*, No. 2, January, p. 12.

Rudnytsky, Ivan L. (1987), 'Pereislav: History and Myth', in Peter L. Rudnytsky, ed., *Essays in Modern Ukrainian History*, University of Toronto Press, Edmonton, pp. 77–89.

Rukh programme (1991), *Prohrama i statut Narodnoho Rukhu Ukrayiny*, Ternopilska oblastna drukarnya, Kiev.

Rumer, Eugene B. (1994), 'Eurasia Letter: Will Ukraine Return to Russia?', *Foreign Policy* No. 96, Fall, pp. 129–44.

Rummel, R. J. (1995), 'Democracies are Less Warlike than Other Regimes', *European Journal of International Relations*. Vol. 1, No. 4, December, pp. 457–9.

Sagers, Matthew J. (1993), 'The Energy Industries of the former Soviet Union: A Mid-year Survey', *Post-Soviet Geography,* Vol 34, No. 6, June, pp. 341–418.

Sauerwein, Brigitte (1993), 'Rich in Arms, Poor in Tradition', *International Defence Review*, Vol. 26, No. 4, p. 317.

Savchenko, Vyacheslav (1995), 'Bessilie vlasti kak priznak krymskoy gasudarstvennosti', *UNIAN-Politika*, No. 14, 4–10 April, pp. 9–10.

Schöpflin, George (1991), 'Nationalism and National Minorities in East and Central Europe', *Journal of International Affairs*, Vol. 45, No. 1, Summer, pp. 51–65.

Schull, Joseph (1992), 'What is Ideology? Theoretical Problems and Lessons from Soviet-Type Societies', *Political Studies,* Vol. XL, No. 4, pp. 728–41.

Shafir, Michael, and Ionescu, Dan (1995), 'The Tangled Path toward Democracy', *Transition*, Vol. 1, No. 1, 30 January, pp. 49–54.

Shmorhun, Oleksandr (1992), 'Pro stari zasadi novoho politichnoho myslennya', *Politolohichni Chitannya*, No. 1, pp. 309–15.

Shtanko, Sergey (1995), 'Stanut li luganskie proletarii pod unsovskiy krest?', *UNIAN-Politika*, No. 24, 13–19 June, p. 68.

Shtyka, Oleksandr (1994), 'Armiya v politychyni systemi ukrayinskoho suspilstva', *Politolohichni Chytannya*, No. 2, pp. 67–83.

Simonsen, Sven Gunnar (1996), *Politics and Personalities: Key Actors in the Russian Opposition*, PRIO Report No. 2, Oslo.

Skorik, Larisa (1992), 'Potreba sinchronnych zusil', *Viche*, No. 9, December, pp. 84–9.

Soldatenko, Valeriy (1993), 'I daty vserosiyskym spravam spokiy', *Viche*, No. 18, August, pp. 125–35.

Stankovcic, Vojislav (1992), 'Problems and Options in Institutionalizing Ethnic Relations', *International Political Science Review*, Vol. 13, No. 4, pp. 359–79.

Stewart, Susan (1993), 'Ukraine's Policy toward its Ethnic Minorities', *RFE/RL Research Report* Vol. 2, No. 36, 10 September, pp. 55–62.

Subtelny, Orest (1991), *Ukraine: A History*, University of Toronto Press, Toronto.

Symonenko, Rem (1994), 'Doktrynu Monro-Mihranyana proholosheno, shcho dali?', *Polityka i Chas*, No. 6, June, pp. 11–17.

Szporluk, Roman (1992), 'The Strange Politics of Lviv: An Essay in Search of an Explanation', in Gitelman, Zvi, ed., *The Politics of Nationality and the*

Erosion of the USSR, St Martin's Press, New York, pp. 215–31.

Talanchuk, Petro (1992), 'Stavka na osobistist, vid traditsii Kyevo-Mohilyanskoyi Akademiyi – do formuvannya tsilisnoyi natsionalnoyi osvity', *Viche*, No. 1, April, pp. 101–12.

Talbott, Strobe (1993), 'The United States and Ukraine: Broadening the Relationship', *US Department of State Dispatch*, Vol. 4, No. 27, 5 July, pp. 480–82.

Tanyuk, Les (1993), 'Ya i My v natsionalnomu postupi', *Viche*, No. 2, February, pp. 116–17.

Tikhii, Sergei (1995), 'Chernoe zoloto iz-za morya Chornovo', *Moskovskie novosti*, No. 9, 5–12 February.

Tilly, Charles (1991), 'Ethnic Conflict in the Soviet Union', *Theory and Society*, Vol. 20, No. 5, pp. 569–80.

Tkach, Vlada (1994), 'Kraini pravi rozrakhovuyut na uspikh u vyborakh do mistsevykh rad', *UNIAN-Politika*, No. 12, pp. 5–6.

Tolpygo, Aleksandr, (1994), 'Resultaty sotsiologicheskikh issledovanii', *Ukrayina Segodnya*, No. 5, May, pp. 64–70.

Tolpygo, Aleksandr (1994), 'Resultaty sotsiologicheskikh issledovanii', *Ukrayina Segodnya*, No. 6, September, pp. 60–65.

Tunander, Ola (1992), 'New European Dividing Lines?', in *Norway Facing a Changing Europe*, conference proceedings, Norwegian Foreign Policy Studies No. 79, pp. 53–6.

Vishnyak, Aleksandr (1995), 'Byudzhet-95: sotsialnie, regionalnie i politicheskie posledstviya', *UNIAN-Politika*, No. 12, pp. 7–8.

Vydrin, Dmytro (1994), 'Naydyem li obshiy yazyk? obyazany', *Viche*, No. 8, August, pp. 68–79.

Vydrin, Dmytro (1994), 'Naydyem li obshiy yazyk? obyazany,' *Viche*, No. 9, September, pp. 60–73.

Vydrin, Dmytro (1994), 'Ukraine on the Nuclear See-saw', *Political Thought*, No. 2, pp. 94–201.

Weydenthal, Jan B. de (1994), 'Poland's Eastern Policy', *RFE/RL Research Report*, Vol. 3, No. 7, 18 February, pp. 10–13.

Wilson, Andrew (1993), 'The Growing Challenge to Kiev from Donbass', *RFE/RL Research Report*, Vol. 2, No. 33, 20 August, pp. 8–13.

Wilson, Andrew (1994), *The Crimean Tatars: A Situation Report on the Crimean Tatars for International Alert*, International Alert, London.

Wilson, Andrew, (1995) 'The Donbass between Ukraine and Russia: The Use of History in Political Disputes', *Journal of Contemporary History*, Vol. 30, No. 2, pp. 265–89.

Woff, Richard (1995), *The Armed Forces of the Former Soviet Union:*

Evolution, Structure and Personalities, Portsmouth, England, Carmichael and Sweet, Vol. 2, Part 2, Section E.

Zagorski, Andrei (1995), 'What Kind of the CIS Would Do ?', *Aussenpolitik*, Vol. 46, No. 3, pp. 263–70.

Zaytsev, Valeriy (1994), 'Khronika sobytiy,' *Ukrayina Segodnya,* No. 5, May, pp. 95–127.

Zaytsev, Valeriy (1994), 'Krymskiy krizis', *Ukrayina Segodnya*, No. 6, September, pp. 123–48.

Zgurets, Sergey (1994), 'Shikuys strunko! Rivnyannya na leitenanta', *UNIAN-Politika*, repr. in *Ukraine Today*, RFE/RL Research Institute, 11 October, pp. 8–11.

Zgurets, Sergey (1995), 'Ukrayina dognala i peregnala vsekh, no s ney, pokhozhe, nikto ne sorevnovalsya', *UNIAN-Politika*, No. 44, 31 October–9 November, p. 34.

Zolotaryov, Volodymyr (1994), 'Odesa yak lokomotiv feodalizatsiyi', *UNIAN-Politika*, repr. in *Ukraine Today*, RFE/RL Research Institute, 13 September, pp. 18–20.

forthcoming...

Laurence Martin and John Garnett

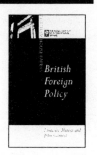

British
Foreign
Policy

British Foreign Policy: Challenges and Choices for the 21st Century

Has the 20th century been one of steady decline for British foreign policy? Indeed, can there be a distinct British foreign policy in an age of regionalism and globalization?

This study challenges the recent perceptions of irrevocable decline and suggests a more balanced assessment of Britain's strengths and weaknesses. This study suggests ways in which Britain could capitalize on its influence and unique assets to promote its interests, and provides a framework for thinking about foreign policy at a time when globalization, multinational companies, NGOs, the European Union and many other new factors increasingly constrain the freedom of government and the traditional role of the Foreign Office.

Professor Sir Laurence Martin was Director of the Royal Institute of International Affairs from 1991 to 1996.

Professor John Garnett is at the University of Wales, Aberystwyth.

176pp
ISBN 1 85567 469 6

April 1997   RIIA/Pinter   Price £11.99 (pb)

forthcoming...

Patricia Chilton

A Common European Defence Policy

With commitments to European defence integration under review at intergovernmental level, this book examines the decision-making processes in the EU and at other European integrative defence relations, including NATO/WEU and defence industrial policy. The author argues that Britain will be faced with managing a 'limited common defence' role with its EU partners, and that this will increasingly be perceived by all the major players as an intrinsic part of transatlantic relations.

This book offers a comprehensive view of both the intentions and the practical experience of security integration, defence cooperation and peacekeeping strategy. It concludes that current developments are not well captured by the language of sovereignty and supranationality. Rather, the important political questions are better addressed within a context of overlapping multiple regimes.

Dr Patricia Chilton is Senior Lecturer in European Politics and Director of the Centre for Research in International Security (CRIS) at the Manchester Metropolitan University.

144pp
ISBN I 85567 509 9

July 1997   RIIA/Pinter   Price £10.99 (pb)

also in this series...

Michael Cox

US Foreign Policy after the Cold War
Superpower Without a Mission?

Contents
- The constrained superpower?

- From geopolitics to geo-economics? Competing in a global economy

- Planning for the next war: restructuring defence

- Strategic alliance or cold peace? Managing post-Communist Russia

- Atlantic rift? The United States and Europe after the Cold War

- Whatever happened to the Third World?

'In this outstanding Chatham House Paper, Michael Cox elegantly and trenchantly analyses America's post-Cold War dilemma.'– *John Dembrell, American Politics Review*

'A splendid account of recent US foreign policy ... shows both the surprising continuities after the Cold War as well as the dramatic shifts from geopolitics to geo-economics ... there is no better book to read on Clinton's foreign policies.' – *Professor Melvyn Leffler, University of Virginia*

'... a clear-headed and thoughtful assessment ... Cox has looked well beyond the headlines to produce the most comprehensive and far-sighted study of this confusing topic so far.' – *Martin Walker, US Bureau Chief, The Guardian*

'No one understands American foreign policy better than Michael Cox, as he demonstrates once again in this informed and stimulating study.' – *Ronald Steel, Professor of International Relations, University of Southern California*

Michael Cox is Professor in the Department of International Politics, University of Wales, Aberystwyth, and Associate Research Fellow at the Royal Institute of International Affairs.

148pp
ISBN 1 85567 221 9

November 1995   RIIA/Pinter £11.99 (pb)

also in this series...

Paul Cornish

The Arms Trade and Europe

Contents

As the world arms market continues to contract, competition for remaining contracts intensifies, and the advantage in the market place is shifting increasingly towards the buyer. Sensing this shift, buyers are more questioning of Western values such as universal human rights and democracy, and more confident in rejecting attempts to link such values with arms and technology deals. Something like a free market in weapons and military equipment has arrived.

The European Union has taken a leading part in post-Cold War attempts to regulate the international arms market. This study draws attention to important differences, as far as the EU is concerned, between trade in finished weapons and trade in manufacturing technology. It examines west European attempts to manage both sides of conventional defence-related trade and evaluates the current obstacles to effective multilateral coordination and regulation.

116pp
ISBN 1 85567 285 5

Dr Paul Cornish is a Visiting Fellow at the Centre of International Studies, University of Cambridge.

December 1995   RIIA/Pinter £10.99 (pb)